FISHERY MANAGEMENT

FISHERY MANAGEMENT

Edited by

Dr. Rabi Narayana Misra

M.Com., LLB., M.Phil, Ph.D.

DISCOVERY PUBLISHING HOUSE PVT. LTD.

NEW DELHI-110 002

Published by:
Namit Wasan

DISCOVERY PUBLISHING HOUSE PVT. LTD.
4383/4B, Ansari Road, Darya Ganj
New Delhi-110 002 (India)
Phone : +91-11-23279245, 43596064-65
Fax : +91-11-23253475
E-mail : discoverypublishinghouse@gmail.com
namitwasan9@gmail.com
sales@discoverypublishinggroup.com
web : www.discoverypublishinggroup.com

***First Edition:* 2016**

ISBN: 978-93-5056-789-0

Fishery Management

Printed at:
Infinity Imaging Systems
Delhi

Preface

From Pre-historic period fishes have been used as Protein rich diet for human beings. The popularity of fishes has been mentioned in our religious literature like the Ramayana and Mahabharata. Fresh water fishes provide valuable source of food supply to the inhabitants of the countries located in tropical regions. Fisheries, including aquaculture provides an important source of protein food, employment, trade and economic well being for the present and the future generation. This resources are assumed to be an unlimited gift of nature.

The problem of 'Protein gap' at present is more acute. The shortage of conventional food aggravates the problem. Producing more sea and water fish resources will definitely support not only the present population of the world as well as India. Besides being used as a good food, fish lever is an important source of oil containing vitamin. Body oil from fish is extensively used in shop industry and tunning. So, fishery management is highly essential in the present time. This book is highly needful for fishery department and the students reading in fisher colleges. It will also helpful to Non-Govt. organizations and to the teachers/students/scholars doing research an fish industry.

—**Dr. Rabi N. Misra**

Acknowledgement

I am thankful to all paper contributors of this book. It is not possible in my part to edit this book without their active co-operation and help.

My wife Smt. Swarna Prava Misra has taken all positive steps for writing this book. My son Roopesh, Rookesh along with my daughter-in-laws Amrita and Bandita were taken all the pain for writing this book.

I convey my thanks and express gratitude to Mr. Tilak Wasan, the Director/Owner of Discovery Publishing House Pvt. Ltd., New Delhi for publishing this book without any hesitation. I am also thankful to his son Mr. Parul Wasan and other members of the staff of Discovery Publishing House for their kind help and co-operation in publishing the book in time.

—**Dr. Rabi N. Misra**

CONTENTS

Fishery Management
Edited by: Dr. Rabi N. Misra
ISBN: 978-93-5056-789-0
Edition: 2016
Published by: Discovery Publishing House Pvt. Ltd.,
New Delhi (India)

The Role of Fishier Sector Development of Indian Economy

Shri G. Chandrayya
Senior Lecturer in Commerce
Government College (A), Rajahmundry

Fisheries Sector

India is the second largest producer of fish in the world contributing to 5.43% of global fish production. India is also a major producer of fish through aquaculture and ranks second in the world after China. The total fish production during 2010-11 (provisional) is at 8.42 million metric tonnes with a contribution of 5.20 million metric tonnes from inland sector and 3.22 million metric tonnes from marine sector respectively. Fisheries being one of the promising sectors of agriculture and allied activities in India, a growth target rate of 6 per cent was fixed by the Union Government so as to achieve the overall growth rate of 4.1 per cent for Agriculture during the 11th Five year Plan. Though there is marginal variation in growth rate of marine fish production the growth rate of inland fish production registered an impressive 5.52 per cent during

2009-10. During 2010-11 the volume of fish and fish products exported was 8,13,091 tonnes worth ₹ 12901.47 crores. As per the estimates of Central Statistical Organization (CSO), the values of GDP from fisheries sector at current price during 2009-10 was ₹ 52,363 crores which is 4.85 per cent of the total GDP of Agriculture and allied sectors.

Fisheries sector occupies a very important place in the socio-economic development of the country. It has been recognized as a powerful income and employment generator as it stimulates growth of a number of subsidiary industries, and is a source of cheap and nutritious food besides being a foreign exchange earner. Most importantly, it is the source of livelihood for a large section of economically backward population of the country. The main challenges facing fisheries development in the country includes accurate data on assessment of fishery resources and their potential in terms of fish production, development of sustainable technologies for fin and shell fish culture, yield optimization, harvest and post-harvest operations, landing and berthing facilities for fishing vessels and welfare of fishermen.

Aspirations

- Enhancement of fish production - at an annual growth rate of 6%.
- Increasing the per capita consumption of fish to 10-11 kg/annum.
- Empowerment and welfare of fishers.
- Capacity building of fishers, fish farmers and fishery professionals and strengthening of infrastructure.
- Creation of marketing facilities with forward and backward linkages.
- Sustainable management of fishery resources.
- Adequate infrastructure in the form of fishing harbours and fish landing centres.
- Increasing employment generating ability of fisheries sector.

- Strengthening of infrastructure including transport, storage and processing.

Inland fisheries and aquaculture

Aquaculture is the fastest growing food producing sector in the world with an annual growth of around 7 per cent. India is the second largest producer of fish both in total and from aquaculture. Increasing the demand for fish and fishery products would be mostly sourced from aquaculture and culture based capture fisheries in reservoirs as capture fisheries growth world over is stagnant. Issues that need to be addressed for enhancing aquaculture production on a sustainable basis are:

- Intensification of aquaculture in ponds and tanks.
- Increase of the productivity of ponds and reservoirs.
- Usage of derelict water bodies.
- Construction of new ponds and tanks.
- Introduction of culture based capture fisheries in reservoirs.
- Species diversification and introduction of high value commercial species.
- Development of breeding and farming technologies for new indigenous species that have potential for farming and market demand.
- Assess the potential impact of already introduced alien species and if found environment friendly, develop suitable management practices for their farming as is being done in the case of *Litopenaeus vannamei and Pangasius sutchi.*
- Small-scale fish farming through cage culture in reservoirs, rivers and irrigation canals.
- Establishment and expansion of fish hatcheries for production of quality fish seed.
- Development and availability of low cost fish feed for different species and farming systems.

- Research on aquatic health management and development of disease resistant strains of fish.
- Production improvement through genetics and biotechnology.
- Encourage fish consumption through awareness on the health benefits of fish and its nutritional security.
- Aquaculture needs to be treated at par with agriculture in terms of water, power tariff, tax benefits, subsidy, insurance and credit.

Marine Fisheries

Harvesting of marine fisheries resources in the country warrants stronger emphasis on invoking technological innovations as well as management paradigms that reconcile livelihood issues with concerns on resource conservation. Global production of fish from marine capture fisheries in the last decade has stagnated gradually and many stocks have been either over exploited or have reached their maximum sustainable yields. Issues that need to be addressed for enhancement of marine fish production are:

- Open sea cage culture of high value fin fishes and shell fishes involving fisher folk as an innovative system that aims to fulfill not only the fascination to farm the seas as a profitable aqua-venture but also as a potential tool for conservation and mariculture.
- Diversification of fishing towards the under exploited deep sea and oceanic resources like tuna, shark, sail fish and allied species.
- Exploitation of perch resources in and around Island waters of Andaman & Nicobar.
- Need to reorient the fisheries management regime for a long-term sustainability of the resources and enhancing the economic efficiency of fishing operations.
- Reduction of fish discards at sea and utilization of such discards for production of value added byproducts.

Important initiatives

- An exclusive body for fisheries development called 'National Fisheries Development Board (NFDB)' was established during September 2006.
- Focused attention on reservoir fisheries through stocking of fingerlings in 3052 reservoirs covering about 15.57 lakhs hectares with an investment of ₹ 104.45 crore. It has been reported that fish production in these reservoirs has significantly increased. High value species like *L. vannamei, Pangasius sutchi,* Tilapia etc., were introduced as a part of diversification.
- Established Coastal Aquaculture Authority (CAA) for regulation of coastal aquaculture activities.
- Aquatic Quarantine facilities for screening of Specific Pathogen Free (SPF) brood stocks of *L. vannamei.*
- Under the Centrally Sponsored Scheme on Inland Fisheries & Aquaculture 8,04,753 Ha of water area has been developed for pisciculture; 9,44,727 number of fish farmers were trained and 13,49,930 number of fish farmers have been given financial incentives under Fish Farmers Development Agency (FFDA) for aquaculture.
- In addition assistance was provided for development of 8000 hectares of ponds and tanks for undertaking intensive aquaculture through National Fisheries Development Board (NFDB), 41,221 ha area has been brought under shrimp culture and 33,999 shrimp farmers have been trained on shrimp farming.
- Established 40 new fish seed hatcheries and 33 hatcheries have been renovated/upgraded.
- *In-situ* pen and cage rearing of fish seed has been taken up in all the States including UTs under recently launched scheme of National Mission for Protein Supplements (NMPS).
- Open sea Cage culture of Marine Fin fish piloted through the Central Marine Fisheries Research Institute and

various high value species like Sea bass, Cobia, Etroplus etc., are being cultured.

- Commercial demonstrations on culture of sea bass and lobsters in 50 cages along Karnataka and Tamil Nadu coasts is proposed.
- With a view to promote production of Sashimi grade Tuna, fish processing facility of National Institute of Fish Post Harvest Technology and Training (NIFPHATT), a subordinate office of Department of Animal Husbandry, Dairying & Fisheries, Ministry of Agriculture at Kochi and Vishakhapatnam has been modernized at an investment of ₹ 2.40 crores and ₹ 1.85 crores respectively.
- Under the Centrally Sponsored Scheme (CSS) on Marine Fisheries seven major fishing harbours (FH), 45 minor fishing harbours and 180 fish landing centers have been constructed and commissioned. Besides, another 25 minor FHs and 16 FLCs are under construction.
- 24 fishing harbors/fish landing centres are being modernized in Karnataka, Kerala, Andhra Pradesh, Tamil Nadu, Orissa and Gujarat at a cost of ₹ 48.92 crores.
- Modernization of 80 wholesale fish markets and 44 retails markets and 45 retail fish outlets and 20 Kiosks with investment of ₹ 95.86 crores.
- A fish net making plant has been constructed by Matsyafed, Kerala through financial support from National Fisheries Development Board (NFDB).
- 1813 Ornamental fishes unit have been established in Kerala, Andhra Pradesh and Maharashtra with an investment of ₹ 10.89 crores.
- Under the Central Sector Scheme on Strengthening of Data Base, Marine census, mapping of water bodies and publication of E-Atlas have been undertaken in 12 States.
- Development of Coastal Fisheries through improved design of craft, motorization of traditional craft and promoting safety at sea.

- The Expert group on Revalidation of Marine Fishery Resource (2011) has revalidated marine resource as 4.41 million metric tonnes.
- Marine fishery census has been completed.

Strategic initiatives and schemes required

(*a*) Enhancement of Fish production and productivity for ensuring sustainability limited to aquaculture sector taking into consideration of major inputs like quality and healthy fish seeds, feed etc., and promising species.

(*b*) Adoption of culture based capture fisheries in reservoirs and under-utilized larger water bodies.

(*c*) Diversification of marine fishing activities to tap the deep sea and under utilized resources, multi-day fishing, species-specific fisheries, utilization of by catch etc.

(*d*) Networking of all line Departments/organizations dealing with fisheries under a single agency.

(*e*) Comprehensive policies for treating Aquaculture at par with Agriculture, and enactment of Marine and Inland Bills.

(*f*) Revamping of FFDAs and involvement of Cooperative Societies and Self Help Groups (SHGs) and ensuring the Socio-economic welfare of fisher folk.

(*g*) Post-harvest, value addition and marketing infrastructure.

Key priority areas

1. Enhance production and productivity of the existing water bodies by developing technologies for intensive culture, integrated aquaculture, broodbank development, creating new hatcheries, nurseries, feed mills, diagnostic laboratories etc.
2. Tap the marine resources in the Exclusive Economic Zone (EEZ) and high seas in a sustainable manner.
3. Create adequate post-harvest infrastructure.
4. To treat aquaculture at par with agriculture.

5. Establish schemes for processing of fish hygienically to produce consumer friendly fish/fish products,
6. All organizations dealing with fish and fisheries should be brought under a single umbrella.

Fishery Resources

MARINE	
Length of coast line (Km)	8118
Exclusive Economic Zone (EEZ) million Sq Km	2.02
Continental Shelf ("000 sq km)	530
Number of Fish Landing Centres	1,376
No. of Fishing villages	3,322
No. of fishermen families	7,64,868
Fisher-folk population	35,74,704
INLND	
Total inland water bodies (lakh ha)	73.59
Rivers & canals (km)	1,95,210
Reservoirs (lakh ha)	29.07
Tanks & ponds (lakh ha)	24.14
Flood plain lakes/derelict waters (lakh ha)	7.98
Brackish water (lakh ha)	12.40

FFDAs & BFDAs (cumulative achievement since inception)

No. of Fish Farmers Development Agencies (FFDAs)	429
Water area covered under FFDA (ha)	8,04,753
No. of Fish farmers trained under FFDA	9,44,727
No. of beneficiaries under FFDA	13,49,930
Average productivity reported (kg/ha/year)-FFDA	2,900
No. of Brachishwater Fish Farmers Development Agencies (BFDAs)	39
Water area covered under BFDA (Ha)	41,221
No. of fish farmers trained under BFDA	33,999
No. of beneficiaries under BFDA	32,524
Average productivity reported (kg/ha/year)-BFDA	1,380

Fish Production

(Lakh tonnes)

Year	Marine	Inland	Total
1991-92	24.47	17.10	41.57
1992-93	25.76	17.89	43.65
1993-94	26.49	19.95	46.44
1994-95	26.92	20.97	47.89
1995-96	27.07	22.42	49.49
1996-97	29.67	23.81	53.48
1997-98	29.50	24.38	53.88
1998-99	26.96	26.02	52.98
1999-00	28.52	28.23	56.75
2000-01	28.11	28.45	56.56
2001-02	28.30	31.26	59.56
2002-03	29.90	32.10	62.00
2003-04	29.41	34.58	63.99
2004-05	27.78	35.26	63.04
2005-06	28.16	37.55	65.71
2006-07	30.24	38.45	68.69
2007-08	29.29	42.07	71.26
2008-09	29.78	46.38	76.16
2009-10	31.04	48.94	79.98
2010-11(p)	32.25	51.98	84.23

(p) Provisional

Fishery Management
Edited by: Dr. Rabi N. Misra
ISBN: 978-93-5056-789-0
Edition: 2016
Published by: Discovery Publishing House Pvt. Ltd., New Delhi (India)

CHAPTER 2

Impact of Pollution on Fishery Management in Odisha

Mrs. Manju Prava Das
Principal
P.G. Dept. of Rural Management
S.M.I.T., Ankushpur

Introduction

Fish and fisheries are an integral part of most societies and make important contributions to economic and social health and well-being in many countries and areas. It has been estimated that approximately 12.5 million people are employed in fishery-related activities, and in recent years global production from capture fisheries has tended to vary between approximately 85 and 90 million tonnes. The products from these fisheries are used in a wide variety of ways, ranging from subsistence use to international trade as highly sought-after and highly-valued items. The value of fish traded internationally is approximately US$40 billion per year. Referring again to data from the 2005 Marine Fisheries Census and CSO (2006), marine fisheries form the livelihood basis for 3.52 million people in over 3,000 villages along the coast. Nearly half of this population is actively involved in fishing and related work such as processing and trade and the majority operate in inshore waters.

The sustainability of fish stocks in Indian waters, particularly for inshore waters, appears uncertain. Over 61 per cent of India's capture fisheries are over-exploited, and most of the remainder are fully exploited with very little prospect for future expansion. Sustaining economic benefits in inshore waters may be difficult. Catch rates and fish exports are declining, the marine fishery is over capitalised by a factor of more than two; the large number of boats not actively fishing clearly point to over-capacity and poor economic returns. While the Government of India is encouraging a shift to more distant deep water fishing in the outer reaches, the majority of fishers operating in inshore waters will continue to face constraints. Fiscal flows from the centre to states for marine fishing are not directly linked to fisheries management but instead mainly support welfare schemes and infrastructure; these subsidies address important socio-economic policy goals, but at the same time, some of the non-welfare subsidies (for boats, gear, nets, fuel, etc.) may be providing the wrong economic signals to inshore producers and can continue to encourage fishing over-capacity.

Fisheries, with its supporting activities, provide a livelihood for millions of people in the Bay of Bengal region. **Odisha** is one of the major state of India both in terms of land area and population-wise. The state is ranked at eleventh position in terms of Population in India. In this state more "than 80 per cent of the population earn their living from agriculture. About 39 per cent of people depend upon fisheries.

Despite the enormous importance and value, or more correctly, because of these attributes, the world's fish resources are suffering the combined effects of heavy exploitation and, in some cases, environmental degradation. Time to time there is seen major impacts on fishing due to the innumerable problems of environment.

Significant environmental degradation has taken place in Chilika Lake in southern Orissa. The main problems here are the large siltation load, causing decreased water exchange with the sea, and the proliferation of weeds in the lake. No significant change in fish catches has yet been demonstrated, but an increase in freshwater species has been observed. Thus, the study is conducted on the Impact of Environment on Fishery Management in Odisha. Mainly the secondary sources related to the study are taken for gathering data.

FISHERIES

There are 329 marine fishing villages in Odisha, with over 20,800 fisherfolk households and a population of 126,000 fishermen, of whom 30,700 are actively engaged in fishing. There are conflicting opinions regarding changes in fish catches and species composition [(Jhingran and Natarajan (1966, 1969); Kowtal (1967); Misra (1988); Mishra and Satapathy (1992)]. The reason for this is probably because there are two opposite processes going on; on the one hand, the increasing inflow of nutrients causes increased production, while, on the other, siltation and reduced salinity cause diminished fish production.

The estimated harvestable potential of marine fish up to 100 m depth is 125,000 t. Based on the MSY estimates made by the Fishery Survey of India (1990), and the current production, it is estimated that an additional yield of 30,000 of fish and crustaceans per annum can be harvested from the continental shelf along the Odisha coast.

The total estimated area suitable for brackish water fish/prawn culture in Odisha is 32,000 ha, out of which approximately 29.000 ha have been surveyed and found suitable. Development has taken place in around 9,000 ha. Fish and prawn production from aqua-culture is shown in the table alongside.

MARINE POLLUTION

Domestic Wastes

Most urban areas have some disposal system and, therefore, a sizeable part of urban wastewater find its way to the natural drainage channels. In rural areas, however, there are no organized systems of water supply and drainage. Most sewage is, therefore, totally absorbed by the soil.

Agriculture

Odisha, a predominantly agrarian state, had a population growth rate of 19.5 per cent in 1981-1991. There is, therefore, pressure on farming activity to increase production. During 1991-1992. 8,490,300 ha were under cultivation *(Statistical Abstracts. 1991).* About 30 per cent of this land was for high yielding varieties, HYV, which, for successful yields, require large amounts of fertilizers, pesticides and insecticides.

Industries

There are major industries in the coastal districts of Odisha. The Brahmani River at Raurkela and in the Talcher Nalco region and the Mahanadi at Brajrajnagar and the Rusikulya estuary near Gopalpur are the most polluted areas of the state. There are reports of fish kill, fall in catches (particularly CPUE) and even in diminished fish quality. Fish caught from the affected areas do not fetch good prices. The entire Odisha coast, particularly at Gopalpur, and the stretch of the Mahanadi river near Brarajnagar are polluted due to heavy metal deposits. Pollution points and points of metal contamination are shown in the Figure on next page.

Treatment of Wastewater

In certain cases, wastewater is diverted into marshes or other detention basins. By physical detention, diversion, filtration and other chemical treatment, the harmful substances are broken down into simpler harmless substances, reducing the intensity of pollution. This is a simple form of what may be called the Effluent Treatment System.

Use of Indusrial/Domestic Wastes

If the cost of effluent treatment could be partly recovered, it would provide an inducement to industries to go in for proper

Map of Odisha showing Pollution Points

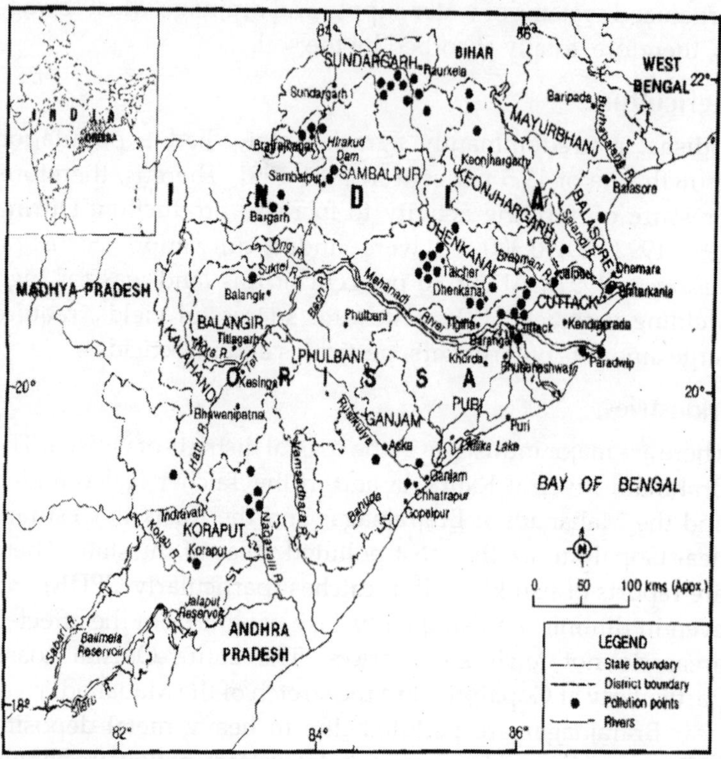

N.B.: The pollution points due to industries and agriculture have been indicated by bullet marks.

effluent management. At least some industries in Odisha have the potential for this. Examples are :

- Use of rice mill effluent in pond fertilization. A rice mill diverts its wastewater tanker to a Sambalpur fish farm. The results are very positive: the cost of pond fertilization is reduced without any environmental repercussions.
- Use of sewage and domestic waste. Sewage from city municipalities is used for fish culture in many places, *e.g.* in West Bengal, which has 130 sewage-fed farms, and in Tamil Nadu.

- Use of pulp and paper mill effluents for irrigation. A paper mill in Odisha has tested irrigation of crops like sugarcane and paddy with paper mill effluents. No adverse effects were reported (Reddy, 1981).
- Use of paper mill sludge. This can be utilized as liming material in agricultural lands and fish ponds.
- Use of sludge from chemical plants. It can be used as binding material in cement manufacturing.
- Use of sludge from sewage. Successful trials have been carried out using sludge as fertilizer at the Berhampur state fish farm.
- Use of fly ash from thermal plants. This can be utilized in brick and cement manufacture etc.

EFFECTS OF POLLUTION

Detrimental effects of pollution have not been recorded in a major way in coastal areas. However, river pollution is much more evident. Since river water finally reaches the sea, and since many fish spend a part of their lives at sea and a part in the rivers, river pollution is also relevant when discussing the marine environment. Among the observed effects are:

- **Biovacuum Zones:** A total destruction of all forms of life, as in parts of the Nandira and Ib Rivers, near Brajrajnagar has been reported.
- **Reduction of fish catch and quality quantum:** This has been noted in the Brahmani, Mahanadi and Rusikulya Rivers.
- **Path-blockages for fish migration**
- **Effects on plankton:** Plankton occurring in the unpolluted zone of Nandira River has diminished with the proportionate increase in pollution load (Tripathy *et al.*, 1990).
- **Depletion of fishery:** The *Hilsa ilisha* and mullet fisheries have been totally destroyed in the Rusikulya estuary.

(Commentaries on water, air pollution and environment protection laws, 1990).

- **Bio-accumulation of heavy metals in fish:** Reported from the Rusikulya estuary and Ib River.
- **Destruction of spawn collection grounds in rivers:** Riverine spawn collection was a thriving industry which attracted a large number of collectors. Spawn collection has now been completely wiped out from the Brahmani River and, to a certain extent, from the Mahanadi River.
- **Freshwater prawn fishery destroyed:** The fishery for *Macrobrachium malcolmsonii* has been destroyed in the Brahamani River (fishermen's report).

CONCLUSION

India's marine fisheries sector makes significant contributions to local and national economic development, trade, livelihoods and environment. There is a strong foundation to build on through an experienced labour force, long history of marine fishing and strong demand for fish products. Thus, the present situation in the Bay of Bengal is not too alarming, but this is no reason for complacency; it only means that there is still time for appropriate action to be taken to, at least, preserve the Bay as it is, if not improve it. Coastal planning must be strictly vetted and rigorously implemented. Ways must be found to curb not only the loss of valuable fertile soils by the side of rivers inland, bul also to prevent these soils making coastal waters turbid and silting estuaries and. lagoons. Better management of fisheries, by preventing overfishing, is also necessary to ensure that the limited resources are sustainable. Hence, timely and effective initiatives are required to be taken in this regard to reduce the problem.

REFERENCE

Banerjee, A.C. and Ray Choudhury, N.C. 1966. Observation on some physico-chemical features of the Chilka Lake. *Indian J. Fish.*, 13: 395- 429.

Das, M.C., Mishra, P.C. Choudhury, K. and Das, R.C. 1985. Bio-accumulation of mercury in River Ib. Reprint. *Ecology and Pollution of Indian Rivers,* pp. 287-299.

Jhingran, V.G. and Natarajan, A.V. 1969. A study of the fisheries and fish populations of the Chilka Lake during the period 1957-65.J. *Int. Fish. Soc. Ind.,* 1:49-126. 1966. Final report on the fisheries of the Chilka Lake (1957-65). *Bull. Cent. Inl. Fish. Res. Inst.,* Barrackpore.

Kowtal, G.V. 1967. Occurrence and distribution of pelagic fish eggs and larvae in the Chilka Lake during the years 1964 and 1965. *Ind. J. Fish.* 14: 198-214.

Mohapatro, P., Singh Samant, N.C.M, Mohanty, D.C. and Bhatta, K.S. 1988. A study of physico-chemical observation of three stations in Chilka lagoon during the year 1985-87. *Proc. Nail. Sem. Conserv., Mgmnt. Chilka.* Dept. of Sci,, Tech. and Env., Government, of Odisha, Bhubaneshwar. (Abstract).

Patnaik, S. and Sarkar, S.K. 1976. Observations on the distribution of phytoplankton in Chilka Lake. *J. Ind. Fish. Soc. India.,* 8: 38-48.

Sarma, A.L.N. 1988. Invertebrate community ecology in the context of conservation and development of Chilka Lake. Dept. of Sci., Tech. and Env., Government of Odisha, Bhubaneshwar. (Abstract).

Fishery Management
Edited by: **Dr. Rabi N. Misra**
ISBN: 978-93-5056-789-0
Edition: **2016**
Published by: **Discovery Publishing House Pvt. Ltd., New Delhi (India)**

CHAPTER 3

Fisheries Management

Dr. Braja Mohan Sasmal
Retd. Prof. of Chemistry,
Sheragada Bungalow
Brahmapur-760 001

Since primitive days the art of catching fishes in the ponds and rivers by the villagers and fishermen for their food supplement was known. Gradually this art of fishing was extended to larger scale and converted to a business or village industry to earn for the livelyhood of the tribe of fisherman who live near riversides or seashores. Since it was a quite profitable business or industry, State as well as Central Government took this business under control and framed certain rules, regulations and acts by making it a national profession or industry of fisheries by exporting the fishes and other fish products to neighbouring states. To streamline the business for the benefit of the fishermen tribe as well as the state revenue, fisheries Management Departments were developed. Fisheries Management, which was day by day reformed and imposed upon the fishing industry in order to control it properly for the benefit of the state.

Modern fisheries management is often referred to as a governmental system of appropriate management rules based on defined objectives and a mix of management means to implement the rules by a system of monitoring, control and surveillance. According to Food and Agriculture Organisation (FAO) fisheries management is the integrated process of information gathering, analysis, planning, consultation, decision-making, allocation of resources and formation and implementation with enforcement as necessary of regulations or rules which govern fisheries activities in order to ensure the continued productivity of the resources and the accomplishment of other fisheries activities.

Starting in the 18th century attempts were made to regulate fishing in the North Norwegian fishery. This resulted in enactment of a law in 1816 on the Lofoten Fishery, which established in some measure what has come to be known as territorial use rights.

The fishing banks were divided into areas belonging to the nearest fishing base on land and further subdivided infields where the boats were allowed to fish. The allocation of the fishing fields was in the hands of local government committees, usually headed by the owner of the onshore facilitates which the fishermen had to rent for accommodation and for drying the fishes. Governmental resources protection based fisheries management after the first over-fishing conference held in London in 1986. In 1957 British fisheries researchers, Ray Bevertanand Sidney Holt published a seminar work project on North Sea commercial fisheries dynamics. In 1960s the work became the theoretical platform for North European Management Schemes.

Political Objectives

According to the FAO fisheries management should be based on political objectives, ideally with transparent priorities. Typically political objectives when exploiting a fish resource are:

(*i*) To minimize sustainable biomass yield.

(*ii*) To maximize sustainable economic yield.

(*iii*) To secure and increase employment.

(*iv*) To secure protein production and food supplies.

(*v*) To increase export income.

International Objectives

Fisheries objectives need to be expressed in concrete management rules. In most countries fisheries management rules should be based on the international rules and regulations, through non-binding code of conduct for responsible fisheries, agreed at a meeting of the United Nation's Food and Agriculture Organisation session in 1995. The precautionary approach it prescribes is typically implemented in concrete management rules as minimum spawning biomass, maximum fishing mortality rates etc. In 2005 the Fisheries Centre at the University of British Columbia comprehensively reviewed the performance the world's major fishing nations against the code.

Management Mechanisms

Many countries have setup Ministries/Government Departments, named "Ministry of Fisheries" or similar controlling aspects of fisheries within their exclusive economic zones. Four categories of management means have been devised regulating their input/investment or output and operating either directly or indirectly.

Technical Means

Different technical means may include:

(*i*) Prohibiting devices such as bows and arrows, and spears or firearms.

(*ii*) Prohibiting nets.

(*iii*) Setting minimum mesh sizes.

(*iv*) Limiting the average potential catch of a vessel in the fleet, electronic gear and other physical inputs.

(*v*) Prohibiting bait.

(*vi*) Snagging.

(*vii*) Limits off fishing traps.
(*viii*) Limiting the number of poles or lines per fisherman.
(*ix*) Restricting the number of simultaneous fishing vessels.
(*x*) Limiting a vessel's average operational intensity per unit time at sea.
(*xi*) Limiting average time at sea.

Catch Quotas

Systems that use Individual Transferable Quotas (ITQ) also called individual fishing quota limit the total catch and allocate shares of that quota among the fishers who work that fishing. Fishers can buy/sell/trade shares as they choose.

A large scale study in 2008 provided strong evidence that ITQ can help to prevent fishing collapse and even restore fisheries that appear to be declined. Other studies have shown negative socio-economic consequences of ITQs, especially on small scale fisheries. These consequences include concentration of quota in the hands of few fishers; increased number of inactive fishers leasing their quotas to others (armchair fisherman); and detrimental effects on coastal communities.

Precautionary Principles

The fishery managers' guide book issued in 2009 by the FAO of the United Nations, advises that "the precautionary approach should be applied when ecosystem resilience and human impact (including reversibility) are difficult to forecast and hard to distinguish from natural changes". The precautionary principle suggests that when an action risks harm it should not be proceeded with until it can be scientifically proven to be safe. Historically fishery managers have applied this principle the other way round; fishing activities have not been curtailed until it has been proven that they have already damaged existing ecosystems. In 2007, in a paper published by Shetzer and Proger, suggested that there can be significant benefits to stock biomass and fishery yield if management is stricter and more prompt.

Fisheries Law

This law is a special branch of law which includes the study and analysis of different fisheries management approaches, including seafood safety regulations and aquaculture regulations. Despite its importance, this area is rarely taught at Law Schools around the world; which leaves a vacuum of advocacy and research.

Climatic Change

In the past changing climate has affected inland and offshore fisheries and such changes are likely to continue. From a fisheries perspective the specific driving factors of climatic change include rising water, temperature, alterations in the nutrient fluxes and relocation of spawning and nursery habitat. Further changes in such factors would affect resources at all levels of biological organizations including the genetic, organism, population and ecosystem levels.

Population Dynamics

Population dynamics describes the growth and decline of a given fishery stock over time, as controlled by birth, death and migration. It is the basis for understanding changing fishery patterns and issues such as habitat destruction, predation and optimal harvesting rates. The population dynamics of fisheries has been traditionally used by fisheries scientists to determine sustainable yields.

The basic accounting relation for population dynamics is the BIDE Models $Ni = N_0 + B - D + 1 - E$.

Where Ni is the number of individuals at a time period (i), N_0 is the number of individuals at a time period (0), B is the number of individuals born, D is number of that died, I is the number that immigrated and E is the number that immigrated between time (0) and time (i). While immigration can be present in wild fisheries, they are usually not measured. Care is needed when applying pollution dynamics to real world fisheries. In the past over simplistic modeling, such as ignoring the size, age and productive status of the fish, focusing solely on a single species ignoring by catch and physical damage to the eco-system based fisheries.

According to Marine Ecologists, Chris Frid, the fishing industry points to pollution and global warming as the causes of unprecedentedly low fish stocks in recent years, writing, "everybody would like to see rebuilding of fish stocks and this can only be achieved if we understand all of the influences, human and natural on fish dynamics". Overfishing has also had an effect. Frid adds, "Fish communities can be altered in a number of ways, for example they can decrease if particular sized individuals of a species are targeted, as this affects predator and prey dynamics. Fishing, however is not the sole perpetrator of changes to marine life-pollution is another example. No one factor operates in isolation and components of the eco-system respond differently to each individual factor".

We propose that rebuilding eco-system and not sustainability per second, should be, the goal of fishing management. Sustainability is a deceptive goal because human harvesting of fish leads to a progressive simplification of eco-systems in favour of smaller high turnover, lower tropic level fish species that are adapted withstand disturbance and habitat degradation.

Elderly Maternal Fish

Traditional management practices aim to reduce the number of old, slow-growing fish, leaving more room and resources for younger, faster-growing fish. Most marine fish produce huge numbers of eggs. The assumption was that younger spawners would produces plenty of viable larvae.

However, 2005 research on rock fish shows that large, elderly females are far more important than younger fish in maintaining productive fisheries. The larvae produced by these older maternal fish grow faster, survive starvation better, and are much more likely to survive than the offspring of younger fish.

Data Quality

According to fisheries scientist Milo Adkison, the primary limitation in fisheries management decisions is the absence of quality data. Fisheries management decisions are often based on population models, but the models need quality data to be effective. He asserts that scientists and fishery managers would be better served with simpler models and improved data.

Ecopath

Eco-path, with Ecoism (EwE), is an eco-system modeling software suite. It was initially a NOAA initiative led by Jeffrey Polovina, later primarily developed at the Fisheries Centre of the University of British Columbia. In 2007, it was named as one of the ten biggest scientific breakthroughs in NOAA's 200 year history. Eco-path is widely used in fisheries management as a tool for modeling and visualizing the complex relationships that exist in real world marine eco-systems.

Human Factors

Managing fisheries is about managing people and business, and not about managing fish. Fish populations are managed by regulating the actions of people. If fisheries management is to be successful, then associated human factors, such as the reactions of fishermen, are of key importance, and need to be understood.

Performance

The biomass of global fish stocks has been allowed to run down. This biomass is now diminished to the point where it is no longer possible to sustainably catch the amount offish that could be caught. According to a 2008 UN report, titled The Sunken Billions: The Economic Justification for Fisheries Reform, the world's fishing fleets incur a "$US 50 billion annual economic loss" through depleted stocks and poor fisheries management.

By improving governance of marine fisheries, society could capture a substantial part of this $50 billion annual economic loss. Through comprehensive reform, the fisheries sector could become a basis for economic growth and the creation of alternative livelihoods in many countries. At the same time, a nation's natural capital in the form of fish stocks could be greatly increased and the negative impacts of the fisheries on the marine environment reduced.

Fishery Management
Edited by: **Dr. Rabi N. Misra**
ISBN: 978-93-5056-789-0
Edition: **2016**
Published by: **Discovery Publishing House Pvt. Ltd., New Delhi (India)**

CHAPTER 4 Problems & Environmental Issues with Fishing in India

Prof. R.N. Misra
Professor in Management Studies,
Berhampur, Odisha
Lt. K. Venkata Rao
Lecturer in Commerce, Government College (A),
Rajahmundry

Many people cite the world demand for seafood and fish as the real culprit for destroying coral reefs, wetlands and ocean beds, but other environmentalist blame the methods and practices of the fishing industry. These practices have devastated the ocean floor eco-systems in many places so that marine and aquatic life can no longer be sustained.

Modifying and Changing Fishing Methods

In order to lessen the impact of commercial fishing and over-fishing that reaches beyond the ocean floor and into entire aquatic eco-systems, a global conservation effort is needed.

Environmental Warning Issued

According to the November 2006 journal issue of Science, the single biggest threat to seafood and fish species around the worldis bad fishing practices. The journal reports that, according to leading marine biologists, if fishing practices are changed, the world's fish and seafood resources will be depleted by the year 2048.

Bad Fishing Practices

Fishing practices have come under scrutiny and determined to be responsible for much of the fish species depletion and degradation of ocean beds. These harmful fishing techniques and practices include:

- **Bottom Trawling:** Trawling along the ocean floor is done with a net. According to a 2005 report submitted to the United Nations Millennium Project, one run of bottom trawling is responsible for the destruction of 5 to 25 per cent of the seabed life.
- **By-catch:** Unintended fish get snared in fishing nets. This fishing by-product is best illustrated by the tuna fishing industry and the by-catching of dolphins. Those concerned by this method of fishing protest by purchasing only dolphin-free tuna, meaning that no dolphins were caught, killed and discarded in the tuna fishing process.
- **Coral Reef Destruction:** *Coral reefs*, the highest biodiversity examples of marine ecosystems, have been destroyed through overfishing methods.
- **Destruction of Food Webs:** One of the worst environmental impacts is when a specific fish species is targeted for harvesting due to high demand. Harvesting large populations of certain species creates an imbalance in the natural prey/predator food chain of marine life. Dynamite and cyanide fishing: These two techniques are illegal in much of the world, but some countries still practice these methods. It's obvious that these techniques leave irreparable damage to the ocean floor and marine eco-systems.
- **Fishing Gear:** The use of environmentally-harmful fishing gear destroys countless ocean beds.

- **Overfishing:** The unregulated amount of fish caught during a season created a fishing industry that was determined to catch as many fish as possible as quickly as possible. This resulted in overfishing and a tremendous amount of dead fish waste.

Marine Conservation to Protect Eco-Systems

One possible solution to the environmental issues created by fishing is marine conservation. There are several steps being taken in an effort to protect and preserve the marine eco-systems through good fishing practices and methods.

Catch Shares

LAPP (Limited Access Privilege Programs) and ITQ (Individual Transferable Quotas) also known as catch shares is a fishing system designed to ensure each fisherman has a share of the season's catch. This regional allotment is known as TAC (Total Allowable Catch). LAPP attempts to control how much fish is harvested in the hope of conservation of the fish population.

Like all allotment systems, most fishermen can sell or buy shares to increase their profits beyond their original allotment. The LAPP systems attempt to eliminate excessive waste, create better fishing practices and allow fishermen to see a higher profit. The LAPP systems removed the competitive nature of seasonal fishing and the urgency for catching as many fish as possible, often resulting in large amounts of dead fish that had to be disposed. Another benefit has been the reduction in the number of fishing boats and destructive gear. By putting the LAPPs in place, the fishing industry believes it has found a way to make fishing a sustainable industry. While there are decided industry issues surrounding the implementation of LAPPs among the fishermen, the side benefit of an improvement in the ocean and sea environs remains controversial.

Creation of Protected Underwater Wildernesses

Protected wilderness areas along the ocean beds and coral reefs, called MPAs (Marine Protected Areas) are helping to rebuild threatened fish species, and populations are on the rise. In addition, these areas are seeing a revitalization of their aquatic and ocean eco-systems. As sanctuaries, all fishing, mining and offshore oil drilling are prohibited.

Wildfishing vs Fish Farms

Another solution to harvesting fish in the wild is fish farms also known as marine aquacultures. Salmon and shrimp are two of the most popular fish and seafood species grown and harvested on fish farms. One of the side-effects of fish farms that can create other environmental issues is the waste product they generate and must be disposed so as not to upset the fish farm eco-system. This is also a controversial environmental issue since the pro is a relief to the overtaxed wildfishing resources while the con is an overstocking in the wild that creates an imbalance among the fish species.

Fish Hatcheries, a Two-Edged Sword

The Pacific salmon was overfished and in 1970, the United States, Japan, Russia and Canada released over 500 million salmon fry into the Pacific Ocean. In 2008, they released over 5 billion more. While these numbers seem astronomical, even "wild" salmon have a low survival rate due to predator culling. The oceans cover two-thirds of the world, yet their feeding grounds are limited. A recent article of the *American Fisheries* Society predicts that when coupled with fish over-population many fish species could starve.

Determining the Severity of Imbalance

According to *Greenpeace*, fish such as marlin, flounder, tuna and other large predator fish species are significantly down, demonstrating an imbalance. This imbalance is also indicated by an increase in other fish species. While there isn't a single solution for the environmental issues created by the fishing industry, conservation appears to be the best approach.

Commercial Fishing: Potential Environmental Issues

Fishing has taken place in the UK for thousands of years. Fisheries are the source of much of our protein and they are of great economic and social importance in communities where the fishing industry is the main employer.

As fishing technology has developed, large-scale commercial fishing has become more widespread. There is now increasing pressure on fish stocks and the marine environment.

Different types of commercial fishing practices can pose different specific threats to the environment. Some of the problems which are a result of commercial fishing are outlined below. You can also find out more about the environmental issues associated with commercial fishing and the EU Common Fisheries Policy on Client Earth's *marine protection pages*.

Overfishing

Overfishing means taking more fish than is sustainable. This is a global problem. By 2009, *over half of the world's stocks were estimated to be over-exploited*. Many stocks have been declining since the Food and Agricultural Organisation's first assessment in 1974. Protecting fish stocks from Over-fishing and maintaining them at sustainable levels is fundamental to securing a sustainable future for the fishing industry.

By-catch

By-catch is the incidental catch of non-target animals during fishing. Animals become hooked or trapped in fishing gear when attracted to the fish in the gear (as bait or target catch) or they are simply unable to avoid accidental entanglement in fishing gear. By-catch can include the capture of dolphins, sea turtles, seabirds, sharks, stingrays, corals, starfish, and non-target commercial fish including juvenile fish and fish with little commercial value. By-catch species can be kept and sold (such as non-target fish) or may be discarded (thrown back into the sea).

By-catch is a key threat to marine biodiversity and it can be avoided by encouraging the development and use of 'selective' fishing gear; that is, special gear design that selects the species being targeted and allows bycatch to escape. Examples include minimum mesh sizes and 'sorting grids' in fishing nets to allow non-target fish to escape, and specially designed hooks that enable turtles to escape. Other avoidance measures such as bird scarers and the use of spatial and temporal fishing measures can also reduce by-catch.

Discards

Discards are the proportion of unwanted by-catch animals that are thrown back into the sea, after they've been caught in fishing gear. Discards usually refers to fish by-catch but it can include other animals caught incidentally.

Most animals that are discarded do not survive after being thrown back into the sea so discarding is a waste of resources as well as a conservation threat. In 2008, up to one third of the total fish catch in UK waters was found to be discarded. However, recent changes to EU legislation (the Common Fisheries Policy, or CFP) will introduce a phased *landing obligation*, or discard ban, for all commercial fisheries in European waters.

Watch a video about discarding and read Defra's information on the *reasons that discarding happens*.

Habitat Destruction

Some fishing activities can also *degrade ocean habitat* and the seafloor which can be damaging to marine eco-systems as a whole. For example, without appropriate management measures the practice of bottom trawling in vulnerable areas can destroy the seabed habitat, which provides shelter and food for a variety of species and which can include complex habitat structures. Important habitats that can be damaged by some fishing activities can include corals (which occur in the UK, not just in tropical areas), sea grass, *maerl beds* as well as important fish spawning and nursing grounds which are essential for fish stock conservation.

Illegal, Unreported and Unregulated (IUU) Fishing

IUU fishing is a serious threat to sustainable commercial fishing. It contributes to over-fishing and can destroy marine habitats. It also means unfair competition for fishermen and operators who do abide by the rules.

IUU fishing is a particular problem in developing counties, where there are limited resources available to control waters and enforce laws.

Fishery Management
Edited by: Dr. Rabi N. Misra
ISBN: 978-93-5056-789-0
Edition: 2016
Published by: Discovery Publishing House Pvt. Ltd., New Delhi (India)

CHAPTER 5

Development of Inland Fisheries in Odisha

Prof. R.P. Sarma
Director,
Institute of Economic Studies,
Brahmapur-760010

Odisha is one of the eight coastal states of India with a coast line of 480 kms along Bay of Bengal and inland water bodies of 9.80 lakh hectors. The state has rivers and canals system of 4,500 kms. Apart from this the state has tanks, lakes and brackish water lakes 9.80 lakh hectors. The total production of fish was 315.59 thousand MTs in 2004-05 which increased to 410.14 thousand MTs by 2012-13, a growth rate of 29.75 per cent in eight years, with an annual growth rate of 3.72 per cent which is not a good growth.

Odisha is one of the States in India blessed with rivers that supplement water needed for agriculture and allied sector activities. There are 7 major river systems in Odisha such as Mahananadi, Brahmani, Baitarani, Budhabalang, Subarnarekha, Rushikulya and Vasandhara. The river systems besides, useful for agriculture, is used for power generation and capture fisheries. Of course these rivers are also cause flood due to heavy rain in catchment area.

Inland production in Odisha is more than the marine production. In the year 2005 the inland production of fish was 193.66 thousand MTs which increased to 291.13 thousand MTs in 2013 an increase of 61.36 per cent in eight years, the annual average growth rate remained at 7.26 per cent, which is almost double the annual growth rate of marine fish production. Production of marine fisheries was 121.93 thousand MTs in 2004-05 and by the year 2012-13 it increased to 118.13 thousand MT.

Inland and marine fish production in Odisha from the year 2004-05 to 2012-13 is presented in Table 1. The growth of inland and marine fisheries is further shown in Fig. 1 which clearly indicates the importance of inland fisheries.

Table 1: Fish Production in Odisha, Figures in 000 MTs

Year	Inland	Marine	Total
2004-05	193.66	121.93	315.59
2005-06	203.23	122.21	325.44
2006-07	213.90	128.14	342.04
2007-08	218.72	130.77	349.49
2008-09	239.30	135.49	375.79
2009-10	253.22	123.33	376.55
2010-11	252.71	133.48	386.19
2011-12	267.53	114.30	381.83
2012-13	291.83	118.31	410.14
Per cent	**71.15**	**28.85**	**100**

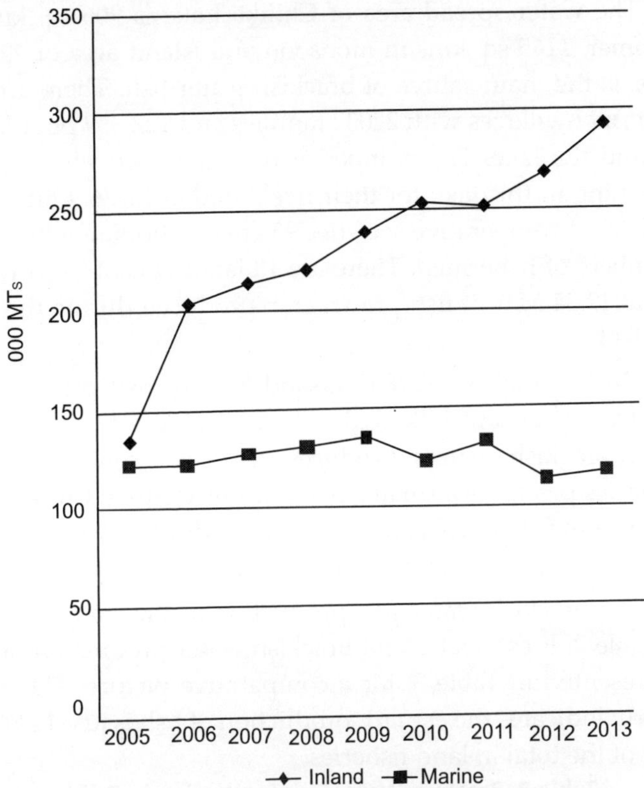

Fig. 1: Growth of Fish Production in Odisha

Chilika Lake

Chilka Lake is one of the potential brackish water systems in the country to produce quality mud crabs (Scylla Serrate and S. tranqueabarica) for live export. More than 200 ton mud crabs are harvested annually at present and about 40-42 tons of larger crabs are exported to overseas markets by Chennai-based crab exporters, valued at about Rs. 1.0 crores. Sea bass (Bhekti) is another economic fish which grows to larger size in Chilka lake and is a much sought after fish in the neighbouring states of Odisha.

The water spread area of Chilika Lake is 906 sq. kms in summer, 1165 sq. kms in monsoon and island area of 223 sq. kms, is the main source of brackish water fish. There are 132 fishermen villages with 22032 families and 122,339 population around the lake. The number of fishermen actively engaged in fishing in this lake for their livelihood is 30936. Out of 104 registered co-operative societies 93 are functioning with 27432 members of fishermen. There are 18 landing centres in which about 12.94 MTs of fish/prawn/crab produced during the year 2013-14.

Out of total of 30.01 thousand MTs of fish produced in brackish water in Chilka Lake alone produces 43.12 per cent, other brackish waters produces 42.02 per cent and small estuaries produces a small percentage of 14.86. In Chilka Lake apart from fish, prawn and crabs are produced on a large scale which has high demand in and outside the state.

The brackish water fish production in the state is shown in Table 2. Fresh water and brackish water production of fish is presented in Table 3, for a comparative picture. The Table clearly indicates the estuary production of fish is just 14.86 per cent of the total in land fisheries.

Table 2: Brackish Water Fish Production in Odisha

[Figures in 000 MTs]

Year	Brackis Water	Chilika Lake	Estuaries	Total Prod.
2009-10	10.97	11.99	2.57	25.53
2010-11	11.62	13.05	3.07	27.74
2011-12	11.97	14.23	3.85	30.05
2012-13	13.23	12.47	4.22	29.92
2013-14	12.61	12.94	4.46	30.01
Per cent	**42.02**	**43.12**	**14.86**	**100**

Table 3: Products of Chilka Lake Figures in Thousand MTs

Year	Fish	Shrimp/ Prawn	Crab	Total
2009-10	7.89	3.85	0.21	11.95
2010-11	7.73	5.04	0.29	13.06
2011-12	7.46	6.41	0.36	14.23
2012-13	7.11	5.03	0.32	12.46
2013-14	7.70	4.92	0.31	12.93
Annual Average Per cent	**7.57**	**5.05**	**0.30**	

Production of fish, shrimp and crab in the Chilka Lake is shown graphically in Fig. 2.

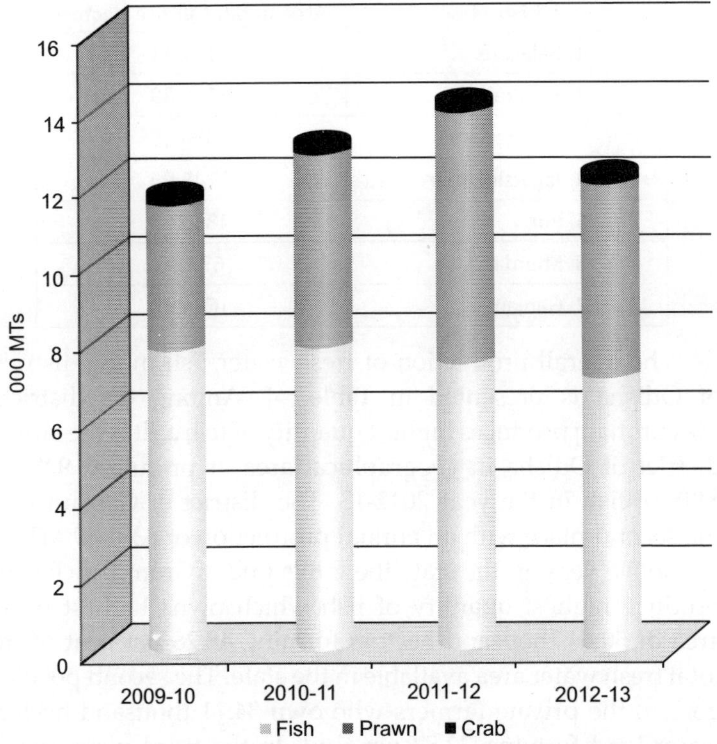

Fig. 2: Products of Chilka Lake

District Scenario

In seven of the coastal districts of Odisha 16.97 thousand hectors of brackish water resources is there which is used for fisheries. The district of Puri has the largest brackish water area in the state comprising of 4.83 thousand hectors followed by the districts of Jagatsingpur and Kendrapara with brackish water area of 3.24 and 2.39 thousand hectors respectively useful for cultivation of fish. In the year 2001 these brackish water area produced 7.07 thousand MTs of fish which forms about 53.04 per cent of total fresh water fish produced in the state.

District-wise brackish water area developed for fisheries up to 2012-13 in Odisha is shown below:

District	Area under Culture Hectors
1. Balasore	2101.11
2. Bhadrak	2100.89
3. Kendrapara	2386.35
4. Jagatsinghpur	3245.06
5. Puri	4833.88
6. Khurda	637.79
7. Ganjam	1664.42

The overall production of fresh water fish in the districts of Odisha is presented in Table 4. Among the districts, Mayurbhanj produces highest quantity of fish as it is the largest district of Odisha in geographical area; it produced 9258.77 MTs of fish in the year 2012-13. The district of Ganjam is in the second place with an annual production of 8381.49 MTs in the above year. In the state the tanks under Gram Panchayars produce highest quantity of fish which owns highest water area of 50.64 thousand hectors forming 48.28 per cent of the total fresh water area available in the state. The second position goes to the private farmers who own 34.11 thousand hectors water land forming 32.52 per cent. In the third place comes the Revenue Tanks owned by the government which posseses

20.16 thousand hectors of fish ponds, forming 19.20 per cent of total water artea available for fishing in the state.

Table 4: Availability of area for fishing in the Districts of Odisha

Area in Hectors

District	GPTank	Revenue Tank	Private Tank	Total
1 Cuttack	1003	400	1405	2808
2 Jajpur	835	205	1310	2350
3 Kendrapada	707	452	2183	3342
4 Jagatsingpur	292	255	1237	1784
5 Puri	4094	170	2391	6655
6 Khurdha	2392	349	913	3654
7 Nayagarh	916	897	768	2581
8 Balasore	1248	261	4285	5794
9 Bhadrak	533	101	1958	2592
10 Mayurbhanj	2250	4697	2310	9257
11 Ganjam	4365	1741	2274	8380
12 Gajapati	1120	3698	154	4972
13 Kandhamal	1350	288	417	2055
14 Boudh	1489	150	525	2164
15 Kalahandi	3838	1113	865	5816
16 Nuapada	655	1629	677	2961
17 Koraput	396	354	464	1214
18 Nawarangpur	673	530	526	1729
19 Malkangiri	349	127	1037	1513
20 Rayagada	423	97	840	1360
21 Sambalpur	2300	568	734	3602
22 Jharsuguda	913	113	213	1239
23 Deogarh	419	80	304	803
24 Baragarh	4224	217	1350	5791
25 Sundargarh	1214	202	1096	2512

	District	GPTank	Revenue Tank	Private Tank	Total
26	Bolangir	4705	152	315	5172
27	Sonpur	3418	327	460	4205
28	Keonjhar	1624	391	1305	3320
29	Dhenkanal	1318	216	1095	2629
30	Angul	1580	384	697	2661
	Total	**50643**	**20164**	**34108**	**104915**
	Per cent	**48.28**	**19.20**	**32.52**	**100**

Import and Export of Fish

For the growing demand of fish in Odisha, the state annually imports on an average 46.60 thousand MTs fish from the neighbouring states, especially from Bihar, Chhatishghar and Andhra Pradesh. On average the annually imports worth around Rs. 41.60 crores. The imports remained as high as Rs. 88.96 crores in the year 2011-12. Odisha also exports fish to the neighbouring states regularly; of course the quantity of exports exceeds the imports slightly over the years from 2008-9 to 2013-14. Quantity imported and export of inland fisheries is presented in Table 5.

Table 5: Import and Export (in 000 MT)

Year	Import from Neighbouring States	Export to Neighbouring and other States
2008-09	17.04	38.39
2009-10	42.06	44.07
2010-11	43.40	37.62
2011-12	59.28	40.29
2012-13	21.21	41.52
2013-14	35.26	45.38
	218.25	**247.27**

The Fishermen Community

Odisha has 813 villages which is frilly inhabited by fishermen community engaged whole time in fishing. There are 1,14,238 fishermen families with a population of 6,05,514. The fishery sector is faced internally with overcapacity, underemployment and low per capita earnings and externally by the lack of alternative occupations, low level of literacy and relatively high levels of debt. The challenge is to develop, in this context, a long-term policy and a perspective plan allowing for the balanced and sustainable management and development of the fishery sector. Fishery sector has an important role for the development of Odisha economy. Production and income of fisherman depends upon various independent variables like—land area, age of the fisherman, hours of fishing, days of fishing, cost of net used, water area in acre etc. On an average fisherman is engaged in fishing for 7-8 months in a year. The monthly income is widely fluctuating due to seasonal variations in catches and other expenses occurring related to fishing. Monthly income from fishing activity varies from Rs.4000 to Rs. 25000.

Fisheries Development Projects

A well planned development policy for the fisheries development will boost not only, the development of rural economy but also accelerate economic growth of Odisha. In the Agricultural Policy of 2008, last formulated by the Government of Odisha, there specified a comprehensive policy for the development of fisheries. In the Eleventh Five Year Plan it was targeted to double the production of fisheries and triple the exports. The state Government has undertaken a massive drive to promote pisci-culture through the Mahatma Gandhi Rural Employment Guarantee Scheme (MGNREGS)

Other development schemes of fisheries carried out by the Government of Odisha are briefly discussed in the following:

Fish Farmers Development Agency (FFDA)

This is a centrally sponsored scheme to develop pond areas and to train fish farmers in modern pisci-culture technique. Up to the year 2010-11, 16.18 thousand hector tank areas have been developed and 50,796 fish farmers were trained about the new techniques of fish farming.

Reservoir Fishery Policy

A Reservoir fishery Policy has been formulated for remunerative pisci-culture in reservoirs. The Fisheries and Animal Resources Development has been empowered to lease out reservoirs to Primary Fishermen Co-operative Societies with an area of 100 acres and above preferably to the displaced and project affected families.

Brackish Water Fisheries Development Agencies (BWFDFA)

The BWFDFAs have been set-up in seven of the coastal districts which have brackish water resources. There are 32.58 thousand ha of water recourses in these districts suitable for prawn culture. The Agencies have developed 15.88 thousand ha prawn culture area by the end of 2010-11. Around 11.63 thousand MT brackish water shrimp was produced during the year 2010-11. Under this scheme 12,422 fish farmers were benefited. Credit was disbursed to the tune of Rs.12.48 crores to the beneficiaries by different banks and the government has provided subsidies to the farmers of Rs. 3.5 3 crores.

Fishermen's Welfare Schemes

There are several welfare schemes for the fishermen community. Chief among them are:

(1) **Accident Insurance Scheme:** Insured fishermen are provided rupees one lakh for accidental deaths and Rs. 50 thousand for partial disability. Cost of this programme is shared by both Centre and State in equal proportions. In the year 2010-11 eight lakh fishermen were covered under this scheme.

(2) **Safety to Marine Fishermen:** Under this scheme life saving jackets is provided at a unit cost of Rs.3 thousand per jacket. Fishermen receiving it has to pay 20 per cent

of cost and the rest is shared by 50 : 50 by State and the Central Government.

(3) **Low Cost Housing Scheme:** This is a centrally sponsored scheme. So far 1989 units of house have been completed. Two community halls and 32 tube wells in the fishermen villagers have been completed. A target have been set to construct 1500 houses for the fishermen.

CONCLUSION

Production of fish is one of the important occupations of village community in Odisha. Even though there is a long sea coast line of 480 kms in the state the inland fisheries production constitutes about 72 per cent of total fish production. The state also exports good amount of fish and fish products to other states. There are good schemes to develop fisheries and fisherman community but so far there is no significant development of fisheries. Fisheries are treated as part of agriculture programme. Now the time has come to take up fisheries as a separate development programmes to boost the rural economy.

REFERENCE

Economic Survey, 2011-12, Planning and Co-Ordination Department, Government of Odisha, Bhubaneswar.

Fishery Management
Edited by: Dr. Rabi N. Misra
ISBN: 978-93-5056-789-0
Edition: 2016
Published by: Discovery Publishing House Pvt. Ltd., New Delhi (India)

Recent Growth of Fishery Sector in Odisha

Dr. S.K. Badatya
Asst. Professor in Finance, MBA,
SMIT, Ankushpur, Bam

Introduction

From pre-historic period fisheries have been used as protein rich diet for human being. In west Bengal, Bihar and Odisha the fish industry is about 1500 years old. In Bengal, every family has at least one pond for fish. The fishing sector in Orissa has not yet fully developed its potential. Orissa ranked 9th in fish production by producing 410.14 thousand Metric Tonnes during the period 2012-13. Orissa has Coastline of 480 kms and continental shelf area of 24,000 sq.km along the Bay of Bengal. This comprises about 6% of the Coastline and 4.7% of the continental shelf area of the country. The state of Orissa having both type of water area like Brackish water of 4.18 lakh ha and fresh water area of 6.73 lakh ha by the end of 2012-13. Chilika Lake is the largest natural brackish water lagoon of Asia. Out of this 218,7 TMT from inland source and remain 130.8 TMT in Marine source. The requirement of fish in the state during 2007-08 is 350.81 TMT basing on nutritional requirement given by WHO, the state has touched 349.48 TMT which is nearing to the targeted figure. The per capita annual consumption of fish in the state during 2012-13 stood at 9.13 kg as against 11 kg recommendation by WHO.

There are two source of fish production. (1) Inland fisheries (2) Marine fisheries. Inland fisheries are classified into two categories one for fresh water fisheries and other for Brackish water fisheries. The fresh water fisheries collected from various sources like tanks/ponds, lakes/swamps, rivers/canals, reserver etc. fresh water fish production was highest in Ganjam district (22.62 TMT) and lowest in Rayagada district (1.04 TMT) during 2007-08. Brackish water fishing Development Agencies have been set-up in seven coastal districts of the state which work for development of brackish water fish farming with special emphasis on prawn culture. The agencies identified 32,587 hectors as suitable for prawn cultivation. State Bank of India is the leading Commercial Bank in the State of Orissa. It is playing an important role in supplying credit to priority sectors. Present scenario financing priority sector plays vital role in contributing a larger share in economic development of the country. In the present study, diet supply to 100 beneficiaries is ₹ 34.27 lakhs.

Odisha, being a maritime state, has considerable scope for the development of inland, brackish water and marine fisheries. The state is endowed with a long coastline of 480 km with continental shelf area of 24,000 sq kms along the Bay of Bengal. It offers tremendous opportunities for development of fresh water, brackish water and marine fisheries with scope of fish production together with employment and income generation for socio-economic prosperity. Fresh water resources of the state are estimated to be 6.75 lakh hectares comprising of 1.24 lakh hectares of tanks/ponds, 2.0 lakh hectares of reservoirs, 1.80 lakh hectares of lakes, swamps and jheels and 1.71 lakh hectares of rivers and canals. The state's brackish water resources are of the order of 4.18 lakh hectares with a break-up of 0.79 lakh hectares of Chilika lake, 2.98 lakh hectares of estuaries, 32,587 hectares of brackish water tanks and 8,100 hectares of brackish water. According to the Fishery Survey in India (FSI), the fisheries potential of Odisha is 5, 13,667 MT. About 4 per cent population (16.26 lakh) depends upon fisheries for their livelihood. Of them, 8.78 lakh depend on inland fisheries and 7.48 lakh on marine fisheries. The fisheries sub-sector contributed about 6 per cent to the GSDP share of the Agriculture Sector for the year 2012-13.

Objectives of the Study

The present study has been undertaken with the following objectives:

1. To examine the trend in growth of fish production in Odisha.
2. To study the progress of export in fish in Odisha.
3. To study the growth of consumption fish during study period.

Methodology of the Study

This study is based on secondary data collected from the various magazine, journal, news papers, Economic Survey, Ph.D. Thesis on fisharies and some web-sites. The period of study covers from 1999-00 to 2012-13. The indicators selected for the studying are growth of production in fish, growth of export during the study period. For evaluation the ratios, percentages have been computed by using data collected from the secondary sources. For proper analysis, some statistical tools like tables, charts, and graphs were also depicted to have a clear vision of the theme of the study.

State Initiatives for Fishery Development

Fishery Development Polic: The fishery development policy has been formulated as a part of the Agriculture Policy, 2008. The main objective of the 12th Five Year Plan is to increase the fish seed production and fish production in order to provide self-employment opportunities which in turn will increase per capita income and eradicate poverty by utilizing unexploited water resources through application of new technologies. During 2013-14, emphasis is being given on the following:

The State Government has formulated the policy for Fishery Development as a part of the Agriculture Policy, 1996. The policy aims:

1. To increase fish production by adopting scientific method of culture.
2. To assist fishermen in more efficient fishing.
3. To boost fishing operation in deep sea.
4. Transmitting technology both for culture and capture to fishermen and farmers.
5. To establish fish feed mills for culture of fish and prawn.

Fish Farmers Development Agency (FFDA): This Centrally Sponsored Scheme is implemented to develop pond areas and to train fish farmers in modern pisci-culture techniques. Total 30 FFDAs, one in each district are functioning. By the end of 2012-13, about 61,173 hectares of tank area has been developed and 53,571 fish farmers were trained through these agencies including development of 518.43 hectares tank area and 750 fish farmers trained in 2012-13 with an expenditure of ₹ 3.46 crore.

Fish Production at National and International Level: The total fish production in different States for the period 2004-05 to 2010-11 is shown in economic survey 2012-13. During 2010-11 West Bengal tops the list with 1,443.26 TMT followed by Andhra Pradesh and Gujurat, Odisha holds 9th position at National Level, produced 386.19 TMT 4.69 per cent of the total fish produced in India during 2010-11. At international level China is the highest fish producing country followed by India, Peru and Indonesia, During 2009 fish production in India stood at 7,845 TMT, about

5.4 per cent of the total fish production in the world (144599 TMT) China produced 49,699 TMT fish which is about 34.4 per cent of the total world fish production during the same year.

Analysis and Discussion

Fish Production and Consumption in Odisha: Fish is a popular food item in Odisha. The State ranks ninth in terms of production produced 4.7 per cent of the total fish production at all India level during 2010-11. During 2012-13, Odisha produced 410.14 TMT of fish of which 291.83 TMT came from inland sources and 118.31 TMT from marine sources. The inland fish production included 261.92 TMT from fresh waters and 29.91 TMT from brackish waters. Crab production has also been increasing over the years. The fish production from Chilka Lake declined from 14.23 TMT in 2011-12 to 12.47 TMT in 2012-13. The State Government has formulated the policy for fishery development as a part of the agriculture policy, 1996.

During 2012-13, fish production in the State was 410.14 TMT, valued at Rs. 3,009.74 crore. The value of fish production has increased by 12.49 per cent over 2010-11 (i.e. ₹ 2,748.44 crore). The value of Inland and Marine fish production has increased by 14.07 per cent and 6.92 per cent respectively during same period. During 2011-12, out of total 381.83 TMT fish production, about 82 per cent were marketed in raw form while 10 per cent were kept for sun drying and salting. The per capita fish consumption in the State is also showing an increasing trend. The per capita fish consumption in the State has increased from 7.7 kg in 2000-01 to 9.13 during 2012-13 as against 11 kg recommended by the WHO. This indicates the improvement of the standard of living and change in dietary pattern of the people of Odisha.

Table 1: Production Fish and Crab in Odisha during the period 1999 to 2013

(Thousand MT)

Year	Fresh water	Brackish water	Marine water	Total	Change from preceding year (in %)	Per Capita Consum-ption	Change from	Crab
1999-00	124.90	10.40	125.90	261.20	—	7.30	—	0.50
2000-01	125.10	13.40	121.10	259.60	– 0.61	7.70	5.48	1.40
2001-02	147.40	20.70	113.90	282.00	8.63	8.10	5.19	1.20
2002-03	154.20	20.00	115.00	289.20	2.55	8.30	2.47	2.20
2003-04	165.60	24.50	116.90	307.00	6.15	8.40	1.20	2.20
2004-05	170.10	23.80	121.90	315.80	2.87	8.70	3.57	1.70
2005-06	179.70	23.50	122.20	325.40	3.04	9.50	9.20	1.40
2006-07	191.63	22.95	128.14	342.72	5.32	8.99	–5.37	1.74
2007-08	195.75	22.97	130.76	349.48	1.97	9.29	3.34	1.79
2008-09	213.00	26.33	135.49	374.82	7.25	13.27	42.84	2.09
2009-10	215.80	25.51	129.33	370.64	– 1.12	10.86	–18.16	2.43
2010-11	224.96	27.75	133.48	386.19	4.20	9.42	–13.25	3.37
2011-12	237.47	30.06	114.30	381.83	– 1.19	10.14	7.64	2.28
2012-13	261.92	29.91	118.31	410.14	7.41	9.13	–9.96	2.35

Source: Economic Survey of Odisha—2012-13.

The Table 1 shows us the details of the fish production and consumption made for the period from 1999-00 to 2012-13 in Odisha. During 2012-13, the production of fish is highest of 410.14 TMT with growth of 7.41%. The production of fish is in increasing trend from 2001-02 to 2008-09 and decrease by 1.12% in 2009-10.12. Similarly, the per capita consumption of fish was also in increasing trend from 1999-00 to 2008-09 except the year 2006-07. Of course there was a falling trend for two years from 2009-10 and 2010-11. This indicates the improvement of the standard of living and change in dietary pattern of the people of Odisha.

Export and Import of Fish in Odisha: As fish production increases in the State, so do its export and import. This trend from 2005-06 to 2012-13 is shown in Table 2. It may be observed that the export of fish is showing an increasing trend over the years except in 2011-12. During 2012-13 about 116.41 TMT fish has been exported from Odisha to other States and foreign countries of which 69.45 TMT (59.7 per cent) were exported from marine sector. Generally marine products like frozen shrimp, frozen H.C frozen pomp ret, ribbon fish, etc. exported to foreign countries like Japan, China, USA, UK, UAE, Indonesia, Hong Kong. Export of frozen shrimps constitutes the major portion about one third of the total marine products exported every year. During 2012-13 about 20,368 MT of frozen shrimp worth of Rs. 878.04 crore has been exported to foreign countries. The trend as regards the import of fish is fluctuating. Import of fish varied from about 21 TMT to 59 TMT per year except for the years 2008-09 & 2009-10 when import shot to 170 TMT and 92 TMT respectively. During 2012-13, about 2,1217 MT of fresh water fish was imported through private trade channels from the neighbouring State of Andhra Pradesh.

Table 2: Export and Import of Fish in Odisha for the period 1999-2013

(In thousand MT)

Year	Marine fish	Fresh water fish	Brackish water fish	Total Export	Change from preceding year (in %)	Total imports
1999-00	69.91	9.98	4.44	84.44	—	42.20
2000-01	61.75	6.26	7.07	75.08	−11.08	41.99
2001-02	60.52	7.57	8.72	76.81	02.30	34.30
2002-03	61.29	7.69	12.58	81.56	06.57	35.71
2003-04	62.96	11.34	14.73	89.03	09.16	34.59
2004-05	65.72	11.72	14.31	91.75	03.05	37.01
2005-06	60.98	13.19	14.85	89.02	−02.98	44.54

Year	Marine fish	Fresh water fish	Brackish water fish	Total Export	Change from preceding year (in %)	Total imports
2006-07	68.00	14.76	14.99	97.75	09.81	38.07
2007-08	71.90	13.18	15.17	100.25	02.56	47.05
2008-09	78.02	21.57	16.82	116,41	16.12	170.42
2009-10	63.02	26.85	17.22	107.09	–08.01	92.07
2010-11	75.72	19.29	18.55	113.56	06.04	43.40
2011-12	55.43	21.49	19.32	96.24	–15.25	59.28
2012-13(p)	69.45	26.34	20.62	116.41	20.96	21.22

Source: Economic Survey of Odisha -2012-13.

The Table 2 shows that the total quantity of fish exported and imported in Odisha during the study period from 1999-00 to 1012-13. Out of 14 years of study only four years export is negatively increased from previous years and remains ten year exports has increased positively from previously years. It indicates that the total export has increased as whole. In the year 2008-09 and 2012-13, the export fish has increased more than 15 per cent from previous year.

CONCLUSION

We conclude from the Table 1 that the growth of fish production is satisfactory so that the consumption pattern fish of the people of Odisha is as also increased. It indicates the improvement of the standard of living and change in dietary pattern of the people of Odisha. Different Self Help Groups(SHGs), NGOs should come forward to help the fishermen to increase their production. Banks and Non-Financial Institutions should come forward to provide loans to purchase modern equipment of fishing's and create saving habits of the people. Another achievement of fishing is increasing of exports which help to cumulate the foreign currencies.

REFERENCES

Directorate of Fosharies, "Orissa Fisheries at a Glance" Government of Orissa, Cuttack.

Dr. Misra & I.P Sahu(2011): Micro Finance for Development of Fisherman, Discovery Publishing House Pvt. Ltd., New Delhi.

Economic Survey of Orissa, 2011-12. Government of Orissa, Bhubaneswar.

Misra, R.N. (2005): Development of Production of Fish in Fresh Water in Orissa", Yojana, (July).

Rao, S.N. (1986): "Fishery Development and Management in India" Pioneer Publishers and Distributiors, Bombay.

Statistical Abstract of Odisha, 2005, Government of Orissa, Bhubaneswar.

Fishery Management
Edited by: **Dr. Rabi N. Misra**
ISBN: 978-93-5056-789-0
Edition: **2016**
Published by: **Discovery Publishing House Pvt. Ltd., New Delhi (India)**

CHAPTER 7

Overfishing Problems of Finance and Recovery in India

G. Chandrayya
Lecturer in Commerce, Government College (A), Rajahmundry
K. Hare Rama Krishna
Lecturer in Commerce, Government College (A), Rajahmundry

What is Overfishing

Overfishing can be defined in a number of ways. However, everything comes down to one simple point: Catching too much fish for the system to support leads to an overall degradation to the system. Overfishing is a non-sustainable use of the oceans.

Below are a few definitions in use by organisations and governments:

> The practice of commercial and non-commercial fishing which depletes a fishery by catching so many adult fish that not enough remain to breed and replenish the population. Overfishing exceeds the carrying capacity of a fishery.

> Catching too many fish; fishing so much that the fish cannot sustain their population. The fish get fewer and fewer, until finally there are none to catch.

> Fishing with a sufficiently high intensity to reduce the breeding stock levels to such an extent that they will no

longer suppport a sufficient quantity of fish for sport or commercial harvest.

What is Causing Overfishing

Worldwide, fishing fleets are two to three times as large as needed to take present day catches of fish and other marine species and as what our oceans can sustainably support. On a global scale we have enough fishing capacity to cover at least four Earth like planets.

On top of the overcapacity many fishing methods are unsustainable in their own way. These methods have a large impact on the basic functioning of our marine eco-systems. These unselective fishing practices and gear cause tremendous destruction on non-target species. By catch/discards and bottom trawling destruction are two examples of this.

Why is Overfishing a Problem

In the first chapter we already discussed that globally fishing fleets are at least two to three times as large as needed to take present day catches of fish and other marine species. To explain why overfishing is a problem we first have to get an idea on the scale of the problem. This is best done by looking at some figures published by the UN *Food and Agriculture Organization.* The FAO scientists publish a two yearly report (SOFIA) on the state of the world's fisheries and aqua-culture. The report is generally rather conservative regarding the acknowledging of problems but does show the key issue and trends. Due to the difficulty of aggregating and combining the data it can be stated that the SOFIA report is a number of years behind of the real situation:

- 52% of fish stocks are fully exploited.
- 20% are moderately exploited.
- 17% are over-exploited.
- 7% are depleted.
- 1% is recovering from depletion.

The above shows that over 25% of all the world's fish stocks are either over-exploited or depleted. Another 52% is fully exploited, these are in imminent danger of over-exploitation (maximum sustainable production level) and collapse. Thus a total of almost 80% of the world's fisheries are fully- to over-exploited, depleted, or in a state of collapse. Worldwide about 90% of the stocks of large predatory fish stocks are already gone. In the real world all this comes down to two serious problems:

- We are losing species as well as entire eco-systems. As a result the overall ecological unity of our oceans are under stress and at risk of collapse.
- We are in risk of losing a valuable food source many depend upon for social, economical or dietary reasons.

The single best example of the ecological and economical dangers of overfishing is found in Newfoundland, Canada. In 1992 the once thriving cod fishing industry came to a sudden and full stop when at the start of the fishing season no cod appeared. Overfishing allowed by decades of fisheries mismanagement was the main cause for this disaster that resulted in almost 40.000 people losing their livelihood and an eco-system in complete state of decay. Now, fifteen years after the collapse, many fishermen are still waiting for the cod to return and communities still haven't recovered from the sudden removal of the regions single most important economical driver. The only people thriving in this region are the ones fishing for crab, a species once considered a nuisance by the Newfoundland fishermen.

Fishing Down the Food Web

It's not only the fish that is affected by fishing. As we are fishing down the food web the increasing effort needed to catch something of commercial value marine mammals, sharks, sea birds, and non-commercially viable fish species in the web of *marine biodiversity* are over-exploited, killed as by catch and discarded (up to 80% of the catch for certain fisheries), and threatened by the industrialized fisheries. Scientists agree that at current exploitation rates many important fish stocks will be removed from the system within 25 years. Dr. Daniel Pauly describes it as follows:

> "The big fish, the bill fish, the groupers, the big things will be gone. It is happening now. If things go unchecked, we'll have a sea full of little horrible things that nobody wants to eat. We might end up with a marine junkyard dominated by plankton."

What can I do to Help

The effects of overfishing are still reversible, that is, if we act now and act strongly.

When fish stocks decline and and fisheries become commercially unviable the damaged stock gets some rest and generally struggles along on a pathetic level compared to it's pre-fishing level, but doesn't go biologically extinc. A damaged system is struggling and shifting, but can still be active (e.g. filled with jellyfish instead of cod).

If we want to we can reverse most of the destruction. In some situations it might only take a decade, in other situations it might take many centuries. Yet in the end we can have productive and healthy oceans again as is shown in many examples around the world. We do however need to act on it now, before we cross the point of no return.

Every long-term successful and sustainable fishery, near-shore or high-seas, needs to be managed according to some basic ground rules:

- **Safe Catch Limits:** A constantly reassessed, scientifically determined, limit on the total number of fish caught and landed by a fishery. Politics and short time economical incentives should have no role in this.
- **Controls on by Catch:** The use of techniques or management rules to prevent the unintentional killing and disposal of fish, crustaceans and other oceanic life not part of the target catch or landed.

- **Protection of Pristine and Important Habitats:** The key parts in eco-systems need full protection from destructive fisheries; *e.g.* the spawning and nursing grounds of fish, delicate sea floor, unique unexplored habitats, and corals.

- **Monitoring and Enforcement:** A monitoring system to make sure fishermen do not land more than they are allowed to, do not fish in closed areas and cheat as less as possible. Strong monetary enforcement is needed to make it uneconomic to cheat.

We need to make sure management systems based on these rules are implemented everywhere. In combination with the banning of the lavish-hidden-subsidies to commercially unviable fisheries.

So, what can I do to help

It's fair to say that individuals cannot solve this global problem all by ourselves, we need politicians to strengthen international law. What we can do is make a difference. Over a decade ago many people started buying dolphin-friendly tuna. Now the time has come to buy ocean friendly tuna. Here are some of the actions you yourself can undertake.

- **Be Informed:** Read up a bit on the issues of overfilshing, have a look at some articles on this site, see if you can find some information regarding your local situation. Keep in mind that while this is a global problem every local situation is different.

- **Know what you eat:** If you eat fish make sure you know what you eat, and pick the ones with the lowest impact. Have a look at the *Guide to Good Fish Guides* for some tips.

- **Spread the word**: I know, it's all rather obvious, hut this is simply how it works. Let your voice be heard!

- Friends: Mention to your friends why you refrain from eating certain fish, tell them about the problems we're facing pointing them to the *Overfishing Basics* at overfishing.org might be a good idea. More material can be found on the *teaching materials* page.
- Elected officials: Write to your elected officials or political party and tell them you are concerned about overfishing and destructive fishing methods. Ask them what they think of the fisheries problem and what they are doing to manage our oceans in a sustainable manner.
- Media: Your local newspaper almost certainly has a section dedicated for letters by readers or articles. If you are motivated writing a letter to the editor is a good way of getting a wide audience.
- Do you have a weblog or website? Write about the state of our oceans and how overfishing is affecting the life of all of us. If you want to link back to overfishing.org there are some *buttons* you can use.
- Students! Have to write a research paper on "something environmental", "an issue that affects you" or "2000 words on a topic of your choice"? Consider the issue of overfishing or the wider issue of the state of our oceans and the various ways humanity is using and polluting it.

Where can I find Answers

This website goal is to be a source of information on overfishing; on its basic problems, specific situations (case studies), progress and solutions. A full *site-map with all articles* is available. Some more information can be found in the teaching materials section. However, for specific or regional fisheries this site is limited as the information available is meant to introduce people to the overfishing issue at large.

If you are interested in a specific or regional fishery a web search is usually the best start. Most countries have local NGO's (Non Governmental Organisations) working on regional overfishing issues. If you have problems finding what you need a forum is available to ask questions. Please don't hesitate to use our *discussion forum on overfishing*!

If you are looking into reading more the book *Cod: A Biography of the Fish That Changed the World* by Mark Kurlansky is a modern classic both on overfishing itself and the social effects it has on communities. The author uses the collapse of the Newfoundland cod stock to give a compelling and accessible introduction to the social parts of the issue. Another good introduction is *The End of the Line: How Overfishing Is Changing the World and What We Eat* by Charles Clover. This book puts the focus on the environmental effects of overfishing.

A list of informative and captivating documentaries on overfishing and destructive fishing (and the social & environmental damages these have) can be found at: *Documentaries about overfishing*.

A Host of Problems

In many cases, fisheries rules, regulations and enforcement measures are not efficient; fishing capacity and efforts are not sufficiently limited or controlled.

Another important issue is that today's fishing activities often occur far from the eye of regulators and consumers.

Current key management problems include:

- **Inadequate Fisheries Regulations:** In many fisheries, current rules and regulations are not strong enough to limit fishing capacity to a sustainable level. This is particularly the case for the high seas, where there are few international fishing regulations.
- **Lack of Implementation/Enforcement:** Even when fisheries regulations exist, they are not always implemented or enforced. For example, many countries have still not ratified, implemented, or enforced international regulations such as the UN Convention on the Law of the Sea and the UN Fish Stocks Agreement. Lack of political

will is also responsible for failures to adopt *by-catch* reduction devices, for example.

- **Lack of Transparency and Traceability:** Customs agencies and also retailers are not always ensuring that the fish entering their country and shops is caught legally and in a sustainable way. As a result, consumers are unwittingly supporting poor management by purchasing fish from unsustainable fisheries. Only when our seafood is traceable can markets and legal systems be effective and reward sustainable practices, whilst deter the irresponsible.
- **Failure to Follow Scientific Advice:** Many fisheries management bodies do not heed scientific advice on fish quotas and set catch limits above the recommended maximum amount; this is the case for *Atlantic cod* and *tuna*, for example.
- **Flag of Convenience Vessels:** Countries are either failing to restrict fishing companies from owning and operating FoC vessels, or are not rigorously inspecting FoC vessels landing at their ports. This include countries with some of the biggest fishing fleets such as the EU, Japan, Korea, and Taiwan (China). This allows illegal, unreported and unregulated (IUU) fishing to continue.
- **Too few no-go Areas for Fishing:** Protected areas and no-take zones, where fishing is banned or strictly regulated, can provide essential safe havens where young fish can grow to maturity and reproduce before they are caught. But just 1.2% of the world's oceans have been declared as Marine Protected Areas (MPAs), and 90% of existing MPAs are open to fishing. The *current lack of protection* is especially worrying for fish spawning grounds and the *deep sea*, both of which are particularly vulnerable to overfishing.

REFERENCES

By-catch: Unwanted marine species caught while fishing for another species. ↵

Discards: Marine species thrown back after capture. Normally, most of the discards can be assumed not to survive. ↵

Dr. Daniel Pauly and others, "Fishing Down Marine Food Webs" SCIENCE Vol. 279 (February 6, 1998), pgs. 860-863. ↵

Fishing capacity: A concept which has not yet been rigorously defined, and there are substantial differences of opinion as to how it should be defined and estimated. However, a working definition is the quantity of fish that can be taken by a fishing unit, for example an individual, community, vessel or fleet, assuming that there is no limitation on the yield from the stock. ↵

Fishing down the food chain: After depleting the most valuable fish we move on the second most valuable fish etc etc. This both involves physically fishing on different locations (from sea mount to sea mount) as well as changing to different, usually smaller, species. Between 1950 and now we systematically worked down our way along the food chain by fishing out all the top predators one after the other. ↵

Fisheries: Policies, Schemes and Incentives ↵

http://www.fishonline.org/information/glossary/ ↵

http://www.lehigh.edu/~kaf3/books/reporting/glossary.html ↵

http://www.reefed.edu.au/home/glossary/o ↵

See the the glossary of marine and fisheries terminology for more definitions of terminology used on this website. ↵

The FAO Fish and Aquaculture organisation http://www.fao.org/fi/default. asp

The State of World Fisheries and Aquaculture (SOFIA) can be found on http://www.Fao.org/sof/sofia/index_en.htm. Figures on this page are taken from the 2006 version of the report. As of 2011 the situation has became worse. ↵

The total amount of fish we take from the system and consume is rising every year. In 2005 we consumed 95 million tonnes of fish. 86 million tonnes of this came from marine fisheries and 9 from inland fisheries. Fish farming accounted for another 50 million tonnes (43%) of production, indirect much of this was fed with the fish from the marine fisheries. In 1980 less than 10 per cent of all fish came from fish farming. ↵

Fishery Management
Edited by: Dr. Rabi N. Misra
ISBN: 978-93-5056-789-0
Edition: 2016
Published by: Discovery Publishing House Pvt. Ltd., New Delhi (India)

CHAPTER 8 Policies, Schemes and Incentives to Fisheries for Economic Development of India

Dr. P. Venkateswarlu
Associative Profesor, Department of Commerce, Andhra University, Visakhapatnam
K. Sujatha
Researcher in Commerce, Andhra University, Visakhapatnam

Both the Central and the State Government have undertaken several policy initiatives and measures to boost the growth of fisheries industry of India. At the Central level, an important policy has been announced as the Comprehensive Marine Fishing Policy, 2004. The objectives of the policy are to:

- augment marine fish production of the country up to the sustainable level in a responsible manner so as to boost export of sea food from the country as well as increase per capita fish protein intake of the masses;
- ensure socio-economic security of the artisanal fishermen whose livelihood solely depends on this vocation;
- ensure sustainable development of marine fisheries with due concern for ecological integrity and bio-diversity; etc.

The policy, thus, advocates protection, consideration and encouragement of subsistence level fishermen. It seeks to promote conservation, management and sustainable utilization of India's invaluable marine wealth.

Earlier, the marine fishing policies focussed only on the developmental needs of the deep-sea sector, leaving aside similar issues pertaining to the coastal sector to the respective marine States/UTs. Even though substantial assistance was channelised through Central and Centrally Sponsored Schemes in to the States/UTs for the development of coastal fisheries, non-exisence of an integrated policy for this sector was found to hamper fulfillment of the national objectives. Therefore, in this present policy, the Goverent seeks to bring the traditional and coastal fishermen also in to the focus together with stakeholders in the deep-sea sector, so as to achieve harmonized development of marine fishery both in the territorial and extra territorial waters of the country.

At the State/UT levle, the fisheries policies have also been framed, from time to time, for integrated development of fishing activities in the country. For example, *State Reservoir Fishery Policy* of Odisha; *Fishery Policy* in Chhattisgarh; etc.

The 'Centrally Sponsored Schemes' for development of fisheries Sector are:

Scheme on Development of Inland Fisheries and Aquaculture: It is a centrlaly sponsored scheme which has been launched to improve the socio-economic status of fishers and other people engaged in the fisheries sector. It covers all inland fishery resources available in the country in the form of freshwater, brackish water, cold water, waterlogged areas, saline/alkaline soils for aqua-culture and capture fishery resources (reservoir/rivers etc.). It is being implemented through the State Governments/UT Administrations. Thus, the components approved under the scheme are:

- Development of Freshwater Aqua-culture: This is an important scheme in inland sector, which is being implemented by a single agency, namely, Fish Farmers Developent Agencies (FFDAs) in the respective States and UTs. Till now, a network of 429 FFDAs has been established in the country. Till 2006-07, about 7.21 lakh hectare water area brought under scientific fish farming through FFDAs. The main objectives of the scheme are to popularise fish farming, create employment opportunities and diversify aqua-culture practices as well as provide assistance to fish farmers, with a view to creating a cadre of trained and well organized fish farmers fully engage din aqua-culture. In order to boost inland fish production, assistance in the form of subsidy is given to the fish farmers for construction of new ponds, reclamation/ renovation of ponds and tanks, first year inputs (fish seed, fertilizers, manures, etc.), integrated fish farming, running water fish culture, establishment of fish seed hatcheries and fish feed mills, etc. Assistance is also given to progressive fish farmers for purchase of aerators to further enhanc the productiity of fish. The expenditure towards developmental activities is being shared on 75 : 25 basis between the Government of India and State Governments. For UTs, Central Government provides cent percent funding assistance.

- Development of Brackish Water Aqua-culture—This scheme has been launched with a view to utilize the country's vast brackish water area for shrimp culture. It is being implemented by 39 Brackish water Fish farmers Development Agencies (BFDAs) set-up in all Coastal States and the UT of Andaman and Nicobar Islands. It is mainly involved in providing technical, financial and extension support to shrimp farmers in the small scale sector. During 2006-07, additional area of about 312 ha was brought under shrimp culture and 500 Fishers were trained in improved practices.
- Development of cold water Fisheries and Aqua-culture in Hilly Regions.

- Development of Water-logged Areas into Aquaculture Estate.
- Productive Utilization of Inland Saline/Alkaline Soils for Aquaculture and Inland Capture Resources (reservoirs/ rivers, etc.).

The last three components are being implemented through the Fisheries Department of the respective States/UTs.

Scheme on Development of Marine Fisheries, Infrastructure and Post-harvest Operations: Under this scheme, the Central Government provides financial assistance to poor fishers through the State/UT Governments for complete development of marine sector. The scheme mainly focuses on motorization of traditional crafts, assisting the small scale mechanized sector by subsidizing the excise duty on fuel, setting up of infrastructure for safe landing, berthing and post-harvest operations, etc. It includes the following components, namely:

- Development of Coastal Fisheries - It has been introduced to improve the socio-economic conditions of the traditional fishermen. It aims to achieve its various objectives through the sub-components, like:
    - Introduction of Intermediate Crafts of Improved Design: This envisages adequate number of appropriately designed boats to judiciously exploit the fishable potential of the country's Exclusive Economic Zone (EEZ). It involves. providing the financial incentives to fishermen groups to take up this new generation craft. The scheme is being implemented through National Cooperative Development Corporation (NCDC). Only cooperatives/group of beneficiaries would be eligible for the assistance. This component on multi-day intermediate class of resource specific fishing vessels in the length range of about 18 meters is to be implemented with a unit

cost of ₹ 40.00 lakhs on which a back ended subsidy equivalent to 10% of the cost restricted to ₹ 4.00 lakhs.

- Motorization of Traditional Craft: It is a scheme, under which the Government provides subsidy to poor fishermen for motorizing their traditional craft as well as for technological upgradation of traditional fishing sector. This aims to help the fishermen to reduce their physical strain and to increase the fishing areas as well as frequency of operation primarily to increase the quantum of catch and earnings of fishermen. The scheme is being continued with the modification that the subsidy benefit will be extended for Out Board Motor (OBM) of 8-10 HP. Further, 50% of the cost of engine is provided as subsidy subject to a maximum of Rs. 20,000 per OBM shared equally by the Centre and the State Governments. In case of UTs, the Centre meets the entire cost of subsidy. It is also being implemented through States/National Cooperative Development Corporation (NCDC).
- Fishermen Development Rebate on HSD Oil: The scheme provides for reimbursement of Central excise duty on HSD Oil used by fishing levels below 20 meter length so as to offset the operational cost incurred by small mechanized fishing boat operators. The cost of Central excise duty on HSD oil at the rate of Rs. 1.50 per litre is subsidized under this component, which is shared on 80:20 basis between the Centre and the States and met fully by the Centre in case of States (which have exempted sales tax fully on HSD Oil) and UTs.
- Safety of Fishermen at Sea: This scheme was introduced to address the issue of safety of fishermen while sea fishing, by installing one Global Positioning System (GPS) and a wireless set on the small-mechanized

fishing vessels of below 20 meter length. It seeks to prevent injury and/or loss of life, fishing boats and implements while fishing as well as make available the early warning system on board.

Development of Deep Sea Fishing: The scheme basically includes two components:

- Resource Specific Deep Sea Fishing Vessels: This component envisages conversion of stern trawlers/ shrimp trawlers to mono-filament long-lining in the form of technological intervention, with a view to meet underutilisation of the existing trawler fleet and of the oceanic tuna and allied species.
- Introduction of VMS: Under this component, Vessel Monitoring System (VMS) has been introduced for initially covering 50 deep sea fishing vessels after conducting a scoping study. The Coast Guard is the implementation agency.

Development of Infrastructure Facilities: This scheme seeks to meet the infrastructure requirements of fisheries sector as well as augment marine fish production and its exports, and includes the following:

- Establishment of Fishing Harbours and Fish Landing Centres: This scheme was introduced with the aim of providing infrastructure facilities for safe landing and berthing of traditional fishing craft, mechanized fishing vessels and deep sea fishing vessels. The facilities created under the scheme are fishing harbours and fish landing centres which includes breakwater, wharf, jetty, dredging, reclamation, quay, auction hall, slipway, workshop, net mending shed and other ancillary facilities.
- Maintenance of Dredger TSD Sindhuraj: Every fish harbour/fish-landing centre is subjected to siltation as a natural phenomenon. Periodical maintenance/dredging is inevitable to keep the harbour/landing centres basin fit for safe navigation. Accordingly, a Trailing Suction Hopper

Dredger 'TSD Sindhuraj' has been procured under the Japanese Grant-in-Aid programme with an aid of Japanese Yen 1248.00 million. This is the most ideal for dredging in shallow waters. The ability of the dredgers with 2.00 to 2.50 meters draft and 200 cubic meters hopper capacity can remove siltation of about 2.00 lakh cubic meters annually. The operation and maintenance of the dredger has been carried out through the Department of Ports, Government of Kerala, for which the capital maintenance cost and insurance etc., is borne by the Centre.

- Development of Post Harvest Infrastructure: This scheme was launched to create facilities for providing remunerative price to the fish farmers for their produce and making available fresh fish at reasonable price to the consumers. Under this Component, State Fisheries Cooperative, Cooperative Federation and primary cooperatives are assisted in strengthen their marketing infrastructure in the shape of fish handling sheds, ice plants, cold storage, retail outlets, etc. It consists of two sub-components: (*i*) developing fish preservation and storage infrastructure; and (*ii*) developing marketing infrastructure such as retail vending kiosks, aqua-shops, insulated/refrigerated vehicles, ice-box, fish display cabinets, visi coolers, etc. This programme is implemented through self-help groups of fisher-women, NGOs, Cooperatives, joint sectors, Government undertakings, and corporations in a location specific manner. The funding pattern is: 100% grant (limited to Rs. 1.00 crore) to Government Undertakings/ Corporations/Federations; 75% grant (limited to ₹ 0.75 crore) to NGOs/Cooperatives/Joint Sector/Group of fisher-women in North East (NE) Region/Hilly/Tribal areas and 50% grant (limited to ₹ 0.50 crore) in general areas; 50% grant (limited to Rs 0.40 crore) to Assisted Sector/Private Sector in NE Region/Hilly/Tribal areas and 25% grant (limited to Rs. 0.25 crore) in general areas.

National Scheme on Welfare Programme for Fishermen, Fisheries Training and Extension: This scheme has been launched to provide financial assistance to fishermen for their welfare as well as provide training and extension support to the fishery sector. It is mainly divided into sub-schemes, namely:

National Scheme on Welfare of Fishermen: This scheme intends to promote welfare programme for fishermen, with its three sub-components:

- Development of Model Fishermen Villages: The objective of the component is to provide basic civic amenities such as housing, drinking water and construction of community hall for fishermen. A fishermen village may consist of not less than 10 houses. The villages would be provided with tube-wells at the rate of one tube-well for every 20 houses. For recreation and common working place, a fishermen village with at least 75 houses is eligible to avail financial assistance for construction of a community hall. Unit costs under the scheme is ₹ 40,0007 for a house, ₹ 30,0007- for the tube-well (₹ 35,000 for North Eastern Region) and ₹ 1,75,0007 for community hall. The expenditure is shared equally between Central and State Government. In case of UTs, the expenditure is fully borne by the Centre.
- Group Accident Insurance for Active Fishermen: The objective of this component is to provide insurance cover to fishermen engaged actively in fishing. Such active fishermen are insured for ₹ 50,000 for one year against accidental death or permanent total disability and ₹ 25,000 for permanent partial disability. The upper limit for insurance premium is ₹ 15 per head.
- Saving-cum-Relief: The objective is to provide financial assistance to fishermen during lean fishing season. Beneficiary has to contribute a part of the earnings during non-lean months. The monthly contributions of marine fishers is ₹ 75 for 8 months, while that of inland fishers is ₹ 50 for 9 months.

Scheme on Fisheries Training and Extension: The main objective of the scheme is to provide training to fishery personnel so as to assist them in undertaking fisheries extension programmes effectively. The scheme provides assistance to fisher folk in upgrading their skills. From the year 2012—2014, this scheme is operated with 80 per cent central assistance in case of States and 100 per cent central assistance in case of UTs and other organizations. Other components of the scheme are to publish manuals to provide adequate extension material, production of video films on the technologies and its publicity, to conduct meetings/ workshops/seminars, etc., of national importance.

Scheme on Strengthening of Database and Information Networking for the Fisheries Sector

This scheme is under implementation with 100% Central assistance. It consists of the following major components:

- Catch Assessment Survey on Inland Fisheries.
- Information Technology Networking.
- Development of Geographical Information System using satellite data.
- Census on important attributes of Marine Fisheries.
- Catch Assessment Survey on Marine Fisheries.

Fishery Management
Edited by: Dr. Rabi N. Misra
ISBN: 978-93-5056-789-0
Edition: 2016
Published by: Discovery Publishing House Pvt. Ltd., New Delhi (India)

CHAPTER 9

Development of Fisheries in the Province of Odisha and Koraput District

Dr. B. Eswar Rao Patnaik
Retd. Sr. Reader & Former Principal, Berhampur

Introduction

A vast segment of population in the province of Odisha live below poverty line i.e. less than $ 1.5 per day. Employment generation is a prerequisite for poverty alleviation from the country. Following globalization experiment in the nineties, organized sector employment opportunities in the country have become thinner. Agriculture is not able to sustain livelihood for workers for more than 6 months in a year. In this context the fishes sector which come under the informal sector occupies a major area in the country and province of Odisha. This paper is the end product of the investigation carried out by the scholar to discuss the potential and prospects of development of fisheries in the District of Koraput and Odisha. Facts and figures furnished on Odisha Province are based on the secondary data while the picture pointed of Koraput district is based on sample survey work of Koraput district conducted by council of Analytical Tribal Studies in 2006-07 (The author was senior consultant to C.O.A.T.S).

Importance of Fisheries

There is substance in the statement that, the fisheries sector widens the employment base of economy by providing full time employment to fisherman. At country level, nutritional security is a jeopardy for many and aqua food are rich sources of proteins, vitamins, calcium and phosphorus, and health boosters of people. The presence of amino acids, Bcomplex vitamins and unsaturated fatty acids in fish kill two birds with one stone, namely ensurance of food security on the one hand and nutritional security on the other to people. Fisheries may provide supplementary employment to people surviving on agriculture in the Khariff season and to that extent inject more income into the body of the economy. A feather to the cap of plan exercises in India is that it is the third largest producer of fish in the world and perhaps the second largest in fish production. Fishery development of the country and the state, has fisheries has bright export market in the world and they attract foreign currency earners.

Fisheries resources are either inland or marine. Rivers their tributaries canals, ponds, lakes and reservoirs are inland fisheries. The sources of marine fisheries are Indian ocean and sizeable number of gulfs and bays along the coast. Fishery development is a state subject.

Potential of Fisheries in Odisha

The State of Odisha has a coastal line of 480 km with continental shelf area of 24000 sq. km. along the Bay of Bengal. The capital-poor state has 1.22 lakh number of tanks/ponds, 2 lakh number of reservoirs 1.80 lakh number of lakes and swamps and 1.71 lakh hectares of rivers and canals. The fisheries potential of the state is 513.667 M.T. as per the Fishers Survey of India. Roughly, 10.84 lakhs people subsist on fisheries of them 7.51 lakhs depends on inland fisheries and 3.33 lakhs on marine fisheries. Fisheries contribute 6 per cent to the 6. D.P share of the agricultural sector for the year 2012-2013.

The welfare Government of India has adopted 2004 marine policy that gives focus on post-harvest operations i.e. maximum utilization of harvested fish for internal consumption and export, minimization of wastes and conformity to international standards. Subsistence level formers are protected by exclusive areas embarked in terms of depth and distance for non-mechanized traditional craft, and area beyond this would be embarked for motorized craft.

Fish Production from Chillika lake increased from 13.7 TMT in 2010-11 to 14.23 TMT in 2011-12. Out of the total rish production, about 85 per cent were marketed in raw form while six-seven per cent were kept for sun drying. The per capita consumption of fish has Increased appreciably from 73 kg in 1999-2000 to 9.91 kg in 2011-12. This implies improvement in the standard of living and change in dietary patterns of the people in the State.

Export and Import of Fish

As fish production increases in the State, so do its exports and imports. This trend, from 2005-06 to 2011-12. Imports varies from about 34 TMT to 59 TMT except in 2008-09 and 2009-10 when imports shot to 170 MT and 92 MT respectively (also see Annexure 3.32). The seafood export sector has been reporting impressive growth during the last few years. The sector reported exports of 21.08 TMT marine products valued at ₹ 792.76 crores during 2011-12.

State Initiatives for Fishery Development

Fishery Development Policy

The Fishery Development Policy has been formulated as a part of the Agriculture Policy, 2008, The main objective of the 12th Five Year Plan is to increase fish seed production and fish production in order to provide self-employment opportunities which in turn will increase the per capita income and eradicate poverty by utilising unexploited water resources through application of new technologies. During 2012-13, emphasis has been on the following:

(*i*) To promote sustainable development of inland fisheries for doubling fish production;

(*ii*) to enhance export earnings;

(*iii*) to enhance contribution of the fishery sector to food and livelihood security of the people engaged in fisheries;

(*iv*) to develop human resources through their capacity building, training and awareness programme.

Fish Farmers Development Agency (FFDA)

This scheme sponsored by the Centre is implemented to develop pond areas and to train fish fanners in modern pisi-culture techniques. There are 30 FFDAs, one in each district. By the end of 2011-12, 60,506.87 ha of tank areas had been developed and 52,821 fish farmers trained, including 469.78 ha tank area developed and 500 farmers trained during 2011-12. Two ongoing schemes, namely FFDA and BFDA, have been merged and renamed as Development of Inland Fisheries and Aqua-culture, under macro- management approach.

The State Reservoir Fishery Policy

The State Reservoir Fishery Policy has been formulated with a view to introducing systematic and remunerative pisi-culture in reservoirs. Hie policy aims at substituting traditional methods by introduction of advanced technologies and techniques. It permits the transfer of reservoirs which have an area of 100 acres and above to the Fisheries and Animal Resources Department, Government of Odisha. The F&ARD Department, Government of Odisha has been empowered to lease out these reservoirs to Primary Fishermen Co-operative Societies registered under the Odisha State Co-operative Society Act, 2001 and preference will be given to displaced/ project affected persons.

Brackish-Water Fisheries Development Agencies (BWFDA)

Chilika Lake with average water spread area of 906 sq. km In summer and 1,165 sq. km in monsoon and island area of 223 sq. km are the main sources of brackish water fish. There are 132 fishermen villages with 22,032 families and 1,22339 population around the lake. The number of fishermen engaged in fishing in the lake is 30,936. Out of 104 registered cooperative societies, 93 are in operation with 27,432 members. There are 27 landing centres at which 13,870 MT of fish/shrimp and 358.26 MT crab landed during 2011-12. BWFDA have been set-up in seven coastal districts which abound in brackish water resources. The State has a total brackish water area of 4.18 lakh ha, out of which 32,587 ha is suitable for prawn culture.

These agencies have developed about 16,387 ha prawn culture area by the end of 2011-12, of which 907 ha have been leased out on a long-term basis. Brackish water prawn culture was undertaken over an area of 4,971.31 ha and 11,975.77 MT brackish water shrimps were produced during 2011-12. By the end of 2011-12, about 13,096 fish farmers benefited and 5,929 farmers were trained in modern shrimp culture techniques. About 674 shrimp farmers have benefited and 211 farmers have been trained on modern shrimp culture technique during 2011-12.

Marine Fisheries

The State has six per cent of the coastline and 4.7 per cent of the continental shelf area of the country. Among six coastal districts, Puri has the longest coastline of 155 km and Bhadrak the shortest, with 50 km. About 114.30 TMT of fish were caught from the marine sector during 2011-12. Out of this, prawn, clupids, catfish and pomfrets are some of the important species. The State has 63 marine landing centres. Odisha Maritime Fishing Regulation Act has been implemented in the State to safeguard the coastal water areas of the State. Registration/ renewal of trawler licenses and conservation of endangered species of fish and turtles have been taken up. The work of

Dhamara fishing harbour has been completed and handed over to Management Society, Dhamara and work at Hatabaredi and Balugaon is under progress.

Fishermen's welfare Schemes

Accident Insurance Scheme

This scheme, which aims at insuring the lives of fishermen, was launched in 1983-84. Rupees one lakh is provided in the event of accidental death or permanent disability and up to ₹ 50,000 is given in the event of partial disability. The cost of this programme is shared by the State and the Centre in equal proportion, in 2011-12, ten lakh fishermen have been covered under this scheme and ₹ 24.50 lakhs was disbursed in cases of disabilities and deaths. It has been proposed to cover 10 lakh fishermen during 2012-13 with a budget provision of ₹ 145.00 crores.

Safety of Marine Fishermen

This scheme is aimed at providing life saving jackets to traditional marine fishermen at a unit cost of ₹ 3,000 per jacket. Fishermen are expected to meet 20 per cent of the cost while 80 per cent is shared by the Centre and State. An amount of ₹ 12.94 lakhs has been proposed towards 25 per cent share during 2012-13 to assist 450 beneficiaries.

Saving cum Relief

Under the scheme, benefit has been given to fishermen during the lean period of fishing and to inculcate the habit of savings among the fishermen. It has been proposed that 17,000 fishermen will be covered during 2012-13 under this programme.

Matsyajitu Unnayan Yojana

This scheme envisages to provide awards to meritorious children of the fishermen community and financial assistance to fisherwomen Self Help Groups (SHGs). It has been proposed to provide scholarships to 100 children of active fishermen and

1,000 fisherwomen SHGs with a proposed outlay of ₹ 100.24 lakhs in 2012-13.

Low cost Housing Scheme under the National Welfare Fund for Fishermen (NWFF)

This is a scheme sponsored by the Centre that envisages better living amenities for poor fisher. Under this scheme, model fishermen's villages are created and low cost housing and drinking water facilities are provided. Since its inception in 1987-88, funds have been allotted for construction of 2,332 houses and 1,989 units have been completed Besides, two community halls have been completed and 32 tube-wells have been installed. Under the scheme, 1,500 low cost homes are targeted to be constructed during 2012-13.

Odisha Pisci-culture Development Corporation (OPDC)

This is the only public sector undertaking in the fishery sub-sector. OPDC aims at carrying on bussiness in pisci-culture in brackish water areas, freshwater ponds and other water sources. It has five hatcheries at Bhanjanagar, Saramanga, Chiplima, Binika and Bayasagar over an area of 103 ha land with a production capacity of 21 crores of spawn and has established 10 million capacity fish-seed hatchery at Kausalyaganga near Bhubaneswar. In 2011-12, it produced 20.50 crore quality fry and sold 18.63 crore fry valued at ₹ 2.63 crores. It also sold 7,300 kg fish worth ₹ 6.58 lakhs. The Corporation has four diesel outlets to cater to the needs of fishermen operating fishing travelers and mechanised boats. During 2011-12, the Corporation sold 11,312 kl of HSD, 20,023 litres of lubricants and 3358 kl motor spirit worth ₹ 70,88 crores and also sold 51 MT net produced in its own net manufacturing unit valued at ₹ 1.89 crores during 2011-12. During 2011-12 the Corporation made a loss of ₹ 2.19 lakh.

Fishfed

Fishfed is an apex body of all Primary Fishermen Cooperative Societies (PFCS) in the State and serves the socio-economic interest and welfare of its members. There are 333 PFCSs comprising of 70,000 fishermen and women members affiliated to FISHFED. The Federation has several businesses including marketing of fish products, providing fishery inputs, leasing fishery sairats in Chilika lake and procuring fish seed.

Fishery Development in Koraput District

Features of the District

The district of Koraput is tribal, industrially backward and is rural oriented with 83.61% of its population live in villages. The district occupies a low rung in the ladder of education *i.e.* 49.2% and its sex ratio is 1046. Grinding and perennial poverty haunts the people of the district around the year for want of livelihood support around the year. As per "District at a glance Odisha 2014" the district has produced 4038.85 million tones of fish in 2012-2013.

Pisci-culture

Water Area available

Fish is one of the cheapest source of animal protein, full of vitamins and minerals. The district has a great potential for fishery development. The inland water available in the district are estimated to be 10,000 ha including G.P. Tanks, revenue tanks and private tanks. Out of 10,000 ha available water area, 6041 ha is estimated to be feasible water area. (PLP, 2008-09), There are four reservoirs *i.e.* Upper Kolab, Jaiaput, Muran and lower Kolab and nine MIPs viz. Kodigam, Jagannath Sagar, Ramgiri, Sabani Munda, Dongariguda, Amda Munda, Damayanti Sagar, Boiragipadar and Bodigaon. The perennial streams like Upper Kolab, Indravati, Machhkund, Janjabati and others are used for capture fishery.

Livelihood for SC/ST

Traditional fishing has been in existence In these reservoirs right from the year of their impoundment. Cooperatives have been organised in most reservoirs having majority of traditional fishermen who belong mainly to SC/ST communities and mostly who are below the poverty line, fishing is their way of life and major livelihood support activity.

Per-capita Availability

However, with a per-capita availability/consumption of only 3.3 km the district is far below the state average consumption of 9.1 kgs. per annum. Against the annual demand of 8243 MT, the total fish production the district was 3297 MT during 2006-07. Thus, there is a need to improve production and supply of fish to meet with the consumption demand.

Infrastructure Support

One Assistant Director of Fishery-cum-Chief Executive Officer of FFDA is the district in-charge of the fisheries sector. He is supported by a JFO, a Superintendent of Fishery, 5 FEOS and 26 other field level and office staff. There is a Government Fish Farm at Jeypore, with the prime objective of catering the fish seed demand of the district. It is the only breeding farm having a Chinese Circular Hatchery, which produces quality spawan and fry to cater to the fry demand of the entire district.

Infrastructural Gap

- The district farm needs strengthening the hatchery. This will enhance the capacity utilisation of the farm.
- The district has only one farm-cum-nursery with a capacity of 80 lakh fry against the demand for 160 lakh fry per annum.
- Organised fish producers community, marketing support, storage, ice factory and the other important necessities.
- FEO's and Demonstrators are to be posted in all the blocks.
- About 50% of the G.P tanks in the district get dried up.
- Training and exposure visit of the fish farmers are necessary to increase the production of fish. These are the areas where all efforts are to be taken to improve the Pisci-culture.

Fisheries

- Development of inland fisheries so as to increase the production of fish by 50% of the end of 2011-12.
- Renovation of Gram Panchayat tanks so as to increase the production of fisheries.
- Increasing cultivable water area in feasible private lands through bank finance made available at affordable rate and proper subsidy facilities.
- Provision of training to progressive fish farmers on scientific method of fish farming with proper incentive to them.
- The Fishery development arranges sufficient fish seeds to meet the demand of the district.
- Promotion of organized fish producers community, marketing support, storage including cold storage.
- Exposure visit of the fish farmers to the neighbouring state to train them on the technique of increasing Fish Production and making it available round the year.
- Strengthening of the Fish Farm Hatchery by enhancing the capacity utilization of the farm so as to ensure timely supply of fingerlings fry.

CONCLUSION

To conclude sensitive administration, political commitment and effective implementation of the ongoing schemes is the need of the hour.

REFERENCES

Comprehensive District Agricultural Plan for Koraput District. October 2008, Council of Analytical Tribal Studies, Koraput.

Economic Survey, 2012-13.

Government of Odisha. Tanuj Bishoy Indian Water Resources Aqua Food Production and Perspectives of Silver Revolution in India "Dynamics of Rural Development" S.N Tripathy (ed), New Delhi.

Rudarn Dutt and K.P.M Sundaram Indian Economy Sultan Chand & Co, New Delhi, 2010.

Fishery Management
Edited by: Dr. Rabi N. Misra
ISBN: 978-93-5056-789-0
Edition: 2016
Published by: Discovery Publishing House Pvt. Ltd., New Delhi (India)

Chapter 10: Finance to Fisheries Sector in India

K. Hare Rama Krishna,
Lecturer in Commerce,
Government College (A), Rajahmundry, A.P.

Lt. K. Venkata Rao
Lecturer in Commerce,
Government College (A), Rajahmundry, A.P.

Introduction

Fishing has been considered as a primary livelihood option since time immemorial, for the occupants of the coastal belt in India, stretching along 8129 km. Fisheries play a predominant strategic role in the economic activity of our country by its contribution to national income, foreign exchange, food and employment. Moreover, it supports the deprived coastal community with sufficient nutritional security which is otherwise unreachable for such segment. Marine fisheries sector produces about 2.71 million tonnes (2006) of fish per annum. About 12.49 lakh fisherfolk operate using diverse types of craft-gear combinations with regional and seasonal variations all along the Indian coastline. The secondary sector provides employment to more than 15 lakh people and another two lakh people is employed in the tertiary sector. It is estimated that fishery and allied activities provide livelihood security to about 30 million people (Sathiadhas *et al.*, 2007).

Economic Significance of Fisheries Sector

Fisheries sector plays an important role as a foreign exchange earner, in addition to contributing to food and nutritional security. It also acts as a principal source of livelihood to people in coastal areas. The customary analysis reveals that in terms of share of fisheries in total GDP over the years, an increase was noted from 0.62 per cent in 1970-71 to 1.18 per cent in 2000-01 that gradually dropped out in the later period. But in terms of absolute value it can be seen that revenue from this sector has increased at a compound annual growth rate (CAGR) of 16.27 per cent during 1970-71 to 2000-01 and later on at a CAGR of 1.52 per cent. Marginalization in terms of share of contribution to GDP may be attributed to dominance of other upcoming sub sectors like IT and industries. This is also rampant from escalating trend in share of fisheries in agriculture, which increased from 1.46 per cent in the seventies to almost 5 per cent during the current decade.

Export Performance of Fish and Fish Products

Exports played a crucial role for development of marine fisheries and socio-economic scenario of coastal rural sector. The infrastructure development in terms of ice plants, preprocessing centres, processing centres, export houses, consequent transport and other facilities along the fishing villages greatly owes to the growth of marine product exports. Seafood business in India is oriented towards international trade. International trade in fish and fish products has been increasing very rapidly in recent decades. Although export played a vital role for development, the WTO regime on exports should be closely watched and parallel development of domestic marketing system, which will act as shock absorbers, should be accorded paramount importance in our future strategies. Fresh fish, once inaccessible to distant locations are now easily available due to vast improvements in handling technologies coupled with advanced transportation facilities and consequent market penetration. About 80 per cent of the catch is channelised through domestic marketing system and the rest for exports.

Socio Economic Milieu - National Perspective

The marine fishery resources of India comprise 2.02 million sq km of Exclusive Economic Zone with a continental shelf area of 4,91,000 sq. km. Amongst the different maritime States, Gujarat has the longest coast line of 1600 km followed by Tamil Nadu (1076 km) and Andhra Pradesh (974 km). There are 641 fishing villages in Odisha followed by Tamil Nadu (581) and Andhra Pradesh (498).

With regard to basic fish landing facilities, Tamil Nadu ranks first with 352 centres followed by Andhra Pradesh (271) and Kerala (178). The marine fisher population is concentrated in the East coast of India (59%) constituting West Bengal, Odisha, Andhra Pradesh and Tamil Nadu (17,50,790). In the West coast, 17 per cent of fishermen population is from Kerala alone. Among the maritime States, fisher population is highest in Tamil Nadu (22%) followed by Kerala. A similar trend is observed in case of distribution of fisher families across the states. An average fisher household in India has a family size of five, ranging from four in AP, TN and Pondichery to six in Karnataka and Daman & Diu.

Income, Inter-sectoral Disparity and Poverty

The pressure for employment in active fishing is increasing more than proportionate to harvestable yield in the open access marine fisheries. The proportion of catch by mechanised sector as a whole increased from 40 per cent during 1980 to 68 per cent in 1997 and again declined to 66 per cent in 2003. At the same time, number of active fishermen depending on mechanised fisheries increased from 1.14 lakh to 2 lakh and again increased to 4.1 lakh respectively during the same period. Among those engaged in the mechanized sector, 75 per cent work in trawl fisheries and rest 25 per cent in other sectors. In case of motorized sector, 50 per cent are engaged in ring seine fishery alone. There is a wide disparity in income between those engaged in different sectors. It may be noted that still non-mechanized sector is providing about 30 per cent of employment in active fishing, yet harvesting hardly 7 per cent of annual landings (Sathiadhas, 2005). Marginalisation of indigenous non-motorised sector by motorized and mechanized sectors frequently creates conflicts among fishers. The number of annual fishing days per worker reveals that level of employment for hired labourers as well as those not having sufficient equipment is low and they are very much underemployed. The seasonal nature of fishery and risk and uncertainties associated with marine fishing entangled fishermen in low-income trap. The poor economic condition coupled with less availability of finance from institutional agencies compel them to sustain with less equipped fishing implements which in turn results in diminishing returns.

Incidence of Poverty

The corner-stones of development agenda of a nation is based on strategies that rests on economic growth, poverty and inequality. In India rising poverty is of great concern and the official estimates of poverty tend to vary very sharply from year to year. According to the results of the 55th round of the National Sample Survey, the percentage of people below poverty line in India decreased from 36 per cent in 1993-94 to 26 per cent in 1999-2000. The vast majority of India's poor, estimated to be anywhere between 320-400 million, live in rural areas. A study by the International Food Policy Research Institute (IFPRI) notes that while overall economic growth has been impressive since the start of reforms in the early 1990s, positive impact on rural poverty was not observed. The failure to reduce rural poverty is attributed to declining public investment in agriculture, which provides a livelihood to 70 per cent of Indians.

The incidence and persistence of poverty in marine fisheries sector can be attributed mainly to open access nature of marine fisheries and unconstrained labour mobility (FAO, 2005). At times labour mobility to fisheries is accentuated by social factors such as caste system prevailing in India. Notwithstanding the above factors there is considerable growth of population within the fishing community and the newer technologies are adopted that pave way to biological and economic over fishing, lesser per capita production stressing the need for efficient fisheries management essentially directed towards sustainable development ensuring distributive justice. The economics of different craft gear combinations and per capita earnings of fishing labour clearly indicates that the people living below poverty line is not less than 60 per cent in the coastal rural sector (Sathiadhas, 2005). It is explicitly clear that the coastal rural people could not get much of the benefits of the economic development taken place in our country since independence. The policies for alleviating poverty in fisheries sector should focus on certain specific points in addition to common measures adopted. The marine inshore fisheries resources are already over exploited and this result in loss of potential resource rents. The capture of these resource rents by appropriate management efforts can add to economic growth in long run. Further increasing adoption of newer technologies coupled with inadequate use of property rights is an important cause of sectoral disparity and inequitable income distribution. The policies pertaining to advent of alternative avocations to fishers by providing awareness, training and initial resource capabilities can do better in the way of providing mobility to other sectors.

Fisheries Sector—An Outlier in the Kerala Model of Development

Fishing villages all along the Indian coast are comparatively backward, synchronized with underdevelopment. Marine fishery sector in Kerala exhibits disparities, both inter-sectoral and intra-sectoral, while existing within the most acclaimed "Kerala Model of Development" with high human development comparable to developed countries not compromising to low per capita income (Kurien, 2000 and Sathiadhas, 2006). Lack of permeation of development efforts to fishing community is tacit in spite of State's overall advancement. Literacy rate in marine fishing villages in Kerala is 73 per cent, far lower than State literacy rate of 90.86 per cent. A paradoxical picture of low level of human development in fisheries sector is underscored by lower sex ratio of coastal fishing villages (979) compared to the State average of 1058.

Demographic Profile

The coast of Kerala extends to 590 km spreading over nine coastal districts, the maximum coastline being shared by Alleppey and Kannur (82 km). Trivandrum district has maximum fishing villages (42) and Kannur with minimum (11). Number of landing centres is found proportionate to fishing villages. Average fisher households per village in the State is 543 while the highest is in Trivandrum (813) and lowest is in Kasargod (299). Maximum fisher population was observed in Trivandrum (24 per cent) followed by Alleppey (17 per cent) and Kozhikode (15 per cent).

Infrastructure Facilities in Fishing Villages

Infrastructure facilities in a village determine the level of development. It was observed that all fishing villages were electrified with health care facilities extending to all villages in terms of 137 community centres and 357 villages, (average distribution being 1.6 hospitals per fishing village). Institutional financing is facilitated by banks and cooperative societies present in the fishing villages. There were 306 banks (average of 1.4 per fishing village) and 381 cooperative societies (1.7 per fishing village). Concentration of banks and cooperative societies was highest in fishing villages in Kozhikode district.

Women in Fisheries

Women play an active role in secondary sector of marine fisheries. In Kerala, almost 50 per cent of the post-harvest activities are undertaken by them. Majority of the total population working in secondary sector (25%) are engaged in marketing of fish followed by labourers in secondary activities (24%). While majority of their male counterparts are engaged in labour in secondary activities, women are mostly involved in marketing of fish (37%) followed by peeling workers (22%). Women involvement is highest in activities like marketing offish (72%), curing/processing (85%) and peeling (95%).

Women employment in the State was highest in Thiruvananthapuram (45%) followed by Alleppey (18%) and Kollam (13%). In Kannur and Malappuram women involvement in secondary activities were hardly one per cent of the total women in the State. Majority of women undertook marketing of fish as an avocation in Thiruvananthapuram, Kollam, Kannur and Kasargod. While in districts like Ernakulam, Alleppey and Thrissur, most of them were involved in peeling.

Institutional Financing to Fisheries in Kerala

Finance plays a crucial role in accelerating any business activity/ economic development and fisheries sector is not an exception. The economic activities of the fishing villages mainly depend upon the availability of credit at reasonable cost to enhance production and income. Credit is vital in all spheres of activities including production, harvesting, preservation, processing, transportation and marketing segments. The credit requirements for fishing activity may be varied depending on the purpose.

Short-term credit: for working capital requirements like repair of vessels or engines and subsistence/emergencies during lean seasons and off seasons, festivals, medical expenses etc.

Medium Term Credit: For Procurement of Fishing Gear, Medical Expenses

Long-term credit: for acquisition of vessels, engines, ice plants, cold storages, processing plants, insulated/ refrigerated trucks, farm/ hatcheries/lifecycle events like marriage, education, medical treatment etc.

The financial assistance in fisheries sector may be widely classified into two depending upon the source of credit, being non-institutional and institutional agencies:

1. The *non-institutional agencies* in credit supply encompasses of private moneylenders, traders, commission agents, friends and relatives.

2. *Institutional financing structure* includes government agencies, commercial banks, co-operative banks, NCDC, NABARD, SHG's and NGO's.

The extent and quantum of indebtedness at a reasonable level of interest sourced out from the organised sector is an indicator of development since availability of finances boost up the economic activity and capital formation in a region. The extent of indebtedness and the average outstanding debt per indebted households are comparatively less among fishermen as per the figures of institutional sources, but the affairs of fisher folk is really grim as they are virtually gripped in the hands of non-institutional agencies, namely money lenders and traders for which legitimate data sources do not exist. The ground level credit flow to fisheries sector in 2008-09 stood at Rs. 1281 crore higher than the previous year and recorded almost four times increase compared with 1997-98.

Banks

Banks finance both capture and culture fisheries. They advance for the purpose of crafts and gears, motorisation of crafts, construction of ponds and hatcheries etc. Fisheries financing are classified under the broad division of agriculture and allied activities that is classified as priority sector lending. RBI stipulates that the quantum of assistance to the priority sector shall be 40 per cent of the total credit granted by the banks, of which share of agricultural allied activities loans shall be not less than 18 per cent.

NABARD is the institutional agency at the national level which undertakes refinancing all agricultural and allied activities. Banks in India can be categorised as follows:

(*a*) Commercial Banks Public Sector Private sector

(*b*) Co-operative Banks

  (*i*) State Co-operative Bank District Co-operative Bank

  (*ii*) A Primary Agricultural Credit Societies

(*iii*) State Agricultural and Rural Development Banks

(*iv*) Primary Agricultural and Rural Development Banks

(*c*) Regional Rural Banks.

Types of Direct Finance

(*a*) *Short-term loans*: for fishery related activities.

(*b*) *Medium and long term loans*: Development of fisheries in all its aspects from fish catching to stage of export, financing of equipment necessary for deep sea fishing, rehabilitation of tanks (fresh water fishing), fish breeding etc.

Interest rate: The interest rate for the loans from commercial banks range between 11 to 16. 5 per cent depending upon the quantum of finance.

Margin money: The contribution of the beneficiary in the project (margin money) ranges from 5-25 per cent of the project cost depending upon the category of the borrowers i.e. 5 per cent for small farmers, 10 per cent for medium farmers, 15 per cent for large fanners and 25 per cent for others.

Security: The loans are provided on the basis of security of movable or immovable properties or on the standing crop.

Repayment period: Repayment period is fixed by assessing the useful life of the asset created and the repaying capacity of the borrower. In fisheries it varies from 4-10 years.

As per the Marine Fisheries Census of CMFRI, 2005, number of bank branches operating in the maritime districts of Kerala has been enumerated. The State average shows that 1968 fisherfolk are served by each branch in a fishing village. It is well-known that lesser the number of population per branch greater the serviceability of the branch. However this is not comparable to population served per branch office at national or state level, since the scope of fisheries census is limited to fisher families in the fishing villages without considering the other population.

Refinance Assistance by NABARD

NABARD supports the fisheries sector mainly by way of refinancing activities. About 90 per cent of the bank loan for all investments under fisheries sector financed by the banks would be refinanced by NABARD. The eligible agencies for refinancing assistance are:

- Commercial Banks
- Regional Rural Banks Co-operative Banks
- Co-operative Agricultural and Rural Development Banks Primary Urban Cooperative Banks

Self-Help Groups Governments

NABARD refinance constitutes 28 per cent of the total ground level credit flow to agriculture and allied activities. During 2008-09, NABARD introduced a product/scheme for supporting small scale Activity Based Groups (ABG) in which capacity building, production/investment credit and market related support would be extended. The scheme focuses on formation and nurturing of groups engaged in similar economic activities such as farmers, fishermen, handloom weavers etc to improve their efficiency of production and realize better terms from the market through economies of aggregation and scale. The scheme operates both on grant and loan modes, where loans would cover investment activities and working capital needs of groups (NABARD, 2009). The refinance assistance to fisheries sector by NABARD is very meager which accounts for only 0.3 per cent of the total refinance disbursed. It is observed that fisheries refinance over the years has been fluctuating widely with highest refinance recorded in 2008-09; constituting 0.7 per cent of the total refinance. This pace could not be maintained during 2009-10 where fisheries sector claimed 0.5 per cent share.

REFERENCES

Arunachalam, R. S, Katticaren, K. , Swarup, V and Kalpana Iyer. (2008): *Enhancing Financial Services Flow to Small Scale Marine Fisheries Sector,* A study for FAO/UNTRS, www. un. org. in

CMFRI. (2005): *Marine Fisheries Census of CMFRI*

Dehadrai and Yadava. (2004): *Fisheries Development, State of the Indian Farmer - A Millennium Study,* Ministry of Agriculture, Government of India

GOI. (2006): *Report of the Working Group on Fisheries for the Eleventh Five Year Plan- 2007-2012.* www. planningcommission.nic.in

Kurien, J. (2000): 'The Kerala Model: Its Central Tendency and the 'Outlier", in Govindan Parayil (eds.) *Kerala - The Development Experience: Reflections on Sustainability and Replicability,* London: Zed Books.

Nabard. (2009): *Annual report 2008-09,* www. nabard. org. in

Sathiadhas, R., Ramachandran C., Vipinkumar V. P and Sangeetha K Prathap. (2007): *Status of fisheries economics and extension research in India: Opportunities and Challenges.* Mohan Joseph Modayil and N. G. K Pillai (Eds.). *Status and Perspectives in Marine Fisheries Research in India,* Central Marine Fisheries Research Institute, Kochi, 404 p.

Sathiadhas, R. (2006): "Inter-sectoral Disparity, Increasing Poverty and Inequity among Coastal Fisherfolk in India". Paper given at Conference on *'Social Science Perspectives in Agricultural Research and Development',* New Delhi, India, 15-18 February 2006.

Sathiadhas, R. (2005): "Policy Issues for Marine Fisheries Management in India", *The Seventh Indian Fisheries Forum,* Bangalore.

Fishery Management
Edited by: Dr. Rabi N. Misra
ISBN: 978-93-5056-789-0
Edition: 2016
Published by: Discovery Publishing House Pvt. Ltd., New Delhi (India)

CHAPTER 11 Inland Fisheries Management and Finance

Dr. H. Srinivasa Rao
Reader in Commerce,
Badruka College of Commerce, Hyderabad

P. Subrahmanyam
Lecturer in Commerce,
Government College (A), Rajahmundry, A.P.

Introduction to Inland Fisheries

The multi-specific nature of many inland fisheries implies the use of reference points derived from some emergent parameters of the fish assemblage in combination with the management criteria selected for that particular assemblage. Within multi-species assemblages such reference points may be the age structure of the catch, the mean length of the fish caught, the relative composition of trophic types, or the presence or absence of key species. At present there is insufficient information to establish such reference points for most systems at any but the most generalized level nor is there much information on the resilience of such fisheries when subject to significant changes in species composition induced by excess effort. It is known that fish populations in fluctuating river systems are very resilient and able to sustain considerable stress from fishing and climatic variations but such resilience should not be assumed for all systems.

In the case of new or exploratory fisheries, States should adopt as soon as possible cautious conservation and management measures, including, *inter alia*, catch limits and effort limits. Such measures should remain in force until there are sufficient data to allow assessment of the impact of the fisheries on the long-term sustainability of the stocks, whereupon conservation and management measures based on that assessment should be implemented. The latter measures should, if appropriate, allow for the gradual development of the fisheries.

The provision of the approach is particularly applicable to development of enhanced fisheries where permanent changes can be produced in the target system both ecologically and socio-economically. Widespread introduction of enhancement techniques should be preceded by a pilot phase in a self-contained water body.

If a natural phenomenon has a significant adverse impact on the status of living aquatic resources, States should adopt conservation and management measures on an emergency basis to ensure that fishing activity does not exacerbate such adverse impact. States should also adopt such measures on an emergency basis where fishing activity presents a serious threat to the sustainability of such resources. Measures taken on an emergency basis should be temporary and should be based on the best scientific evidence available.

Inland fisheries are particularly susceptible to natural climatic variations. Large rivers, many lakes and swamps all respond to intra- and inter-annual variation in rainfall. Normally the fish species and assemblages inhabiting such systems have evolved mechanisms to deal with these fluctuation and the greater stress for such systems often arises when the variability is suppressed. However, despite the natural resilience the addition of further stresses at critical times such as during severe droughts may exceed the capacity of certain species or communities to resist and emergency limitations on access, certain types of gear or certain seasons may be contemplated at such times.

Management Measures

States should ensure that the level of fishing permitted is commensurate with the state of fisheries resources.

States should adopt measures to ensure that no vessel be allowed to fish unless so authorized, in a manner consistent with international law for the high seas or in conformity with national legislation within areas of national jurisdiction.

Where excess fishing capacity exists, mechanisms should be established to reduce capacity to levels commensurate with the sustainable use of fisheries resources so as to ensure that fishers operate under economic conditions that promote responsible fisheries. Such mechanisms should include monitoring the capacity of fishing fleets.

The basic fishing unit: The major fishing unit in inland waters centres around the fishers who is the licence holder in most fisheries and who is assigned rights either by government or by acquisition through auction in others. Except in a few major fisheries, such as the Amazon, fishing vessels are small and fishing is often carried out from structures other than boats such as the shore, barrier traps or fixed rafts. Control of effort in inland fisheries is best achieved through the establishment of clear access rights among inland water fishers and fishing communities and the setting up of appropriate mechanisms for ensuring that such access is respected.

The performance of all existing fishing gear, methods and practices should be examined and measures taken to ensure that fishing gear, methods and practices which are not consistent with responsible fishing are phased out and replaced with more acceptable alternatives. In this process, particular attention should be given to the impact of such measures on fishing communities, including their ability to exploit the resource.

Value of multi-gear fisheries: Inland fisheries, especially in rivers and swamps, generally use a wide range of gear (see article 6.6) which enables the fishery as a whole to respond to changing conditions throughout the yearly cycle. Different types of gear are associated with different sections of the fishing community and many inland fisheries consist of complex associations of sub-fisheries. In this respect efforts have to be made to rationalize the use of gear by banning the most damaging - (see article 7. 2. 2 section (g)) - while at the same time conserving social equity. Particular attention should be paid to specialist fisheries which have a potential to damage resources, such as the fisheries for fry for stocking or those for small ornamental species.

States and fisheries management organizations and arrangements should regulate fishing in such a way as to avoid the risk of conflict among fishers using different vessels, gear and fishing methods.

Conflicts between recreational and food fisheries: Substantial conflicts exist between various objectives for managing of inland fisheries. A major difference in resource allocation is between recreational and food fisheries. Because the recreational fishery is generally worth more than the food fishery and because of the lack of secure rights on the part of the food fishers there is a tendency for recreational interests to drive out artisanal and even subsistence fisheries even in countries with food deficits. This phenomenon used to be confined to the affluent temperate regions but is increasing even in less affluent tropical regions.

Conflicts within food fisheries: Fisheries in inland waters are technically and socially complex. The wide variety of gears current in rivers and in many lakes have been developed to catch a wide variety of species and life stages and to be used in different localities and seasons. These various types of gear are usually confined to distinct groups of fishers with the most affluent using the most effective, costly and sophisticated, such as large barrier traps, beach seines or brush parks. Poorer fishers are usually confined to simpler gears such as dip nets, hooks and simple traps. The various categories of fishers may be organized into a harmonious social hierarchy but in other areas they are in direct competition. Care has to be taken in defining fishing policies so that social equity is maintained and that the poorer fishers are not victimized by gear restrictions.

When deciding on the use, conservation and management of fisheries resources, due recognition should be given, as appropriate, in accordance with national laws and regulations, to the traditional practices, needs and interests of indigenous people and local fishing communities which are highly dependent on fishery resources for their livelihood.

Role of indigenous peoples in inland fisheries: Fishing is one of the major activities of local peoples in many areas of the world and has been retained in many areas through long standing traditions. In other areas where indigenous peoples are in reserves they hold the sole rights of access to the fishery. In other areas, particularly where impacts of major dams have eliminated runs of anadromous species, stocking and rehabilitation have been programmed to provide for continuity of the resource.

In the evaluation of alternative conservation and management measures, their cost-effectiveness and social impact should be considered.

The efficacy of conservation and management measures and their possible interactions should be kept under continuous review. Such measures should, as appropriate, be revised or abolished in the light of new information.

States should take appropriate measures to minimize waste, discards, catch by lost or abandoned gear, catch of non-target species, both fish and non-fish species, and negative impacts on associated or dependent species, in particular endangered species. Where appropriate, such measures may include technical measures related to fish size, mesh size or gear, discards, closed seasons and areas and zones reserved for selected fisheries, particularly artisanal fisheries. Such measures should be applied, where appropriate, to protect juveniles and spawners. States and subregional or regional fisheries management organizations and arrangements should promote, to the extent practicable, the development and use of selective, environmentally safe and cost effective gear and techniques.

States and subregional and regional fisheries management organizations and arrangements, in the framework of their respective competences, should introduce measures for depleted resources and those resources threatened with depletion that facilitate the sustained recovery of such stocks. They should make every effort to ensure that resources and habitats critical to the well-being of such resources which have been adversely affected by fishing or other human activities are restored.

Mitigation: Where there are impacts by a non-fishery user which will continue mitigation can only be within the constraints imposed by that use. Repeated inputs are usually to work against the destructive trend of the imposed use. As such, mitigation is of itself rarely sustainable but may contribute to the sustainability of the stock as a whole. Stocks of individual species or groups of species which are either endangered by environmental change or are overfished can be maintained by:

(*i*) attempting to rectify the element in the environment that is limiting such as lack of spawning substrate, interruption of migratory pathways or lack of critical flows;

(*ii*) appropriate stocking programmes;

(*iii*) construction of effluent treatment plants to ensure adequate water quality.

Alternatively, other species may be introduced to the system which are more suited to the altered conditions as in reservoirs in basins where no suitable lacustrine elements exist in the native fauna.

Rehabilitation: Where pressures from other users are eased there may be a possibility to restore natural or quasi-natural features to the river. In contrast to the sustained inputs generally required for mitigation, rehabilitation requires a one off investment after which natural processes should maintain the system. Of course in most rivers regulation and modification will persist elsewhere in the system and thus fully natural regimes will not reestablish. This is particularly true of erosion-deposition processes and it may always be necessary to intervene with such operations as dredging to dispose of material which the modified flow regimes cannot handle. Rehabilitation aims mainly to restore the system to as near pristine conditions as possible through—

Abiotically

(*i*) restoration of channel diversity;

(*ii*) restoration of longitudinal connectivity and

(*iii*) restoration of lateral connectivity.

Biotically

(*i*) stocking

(*ii*) biomanipulation

Restoration of Channel Diversity

Channels of rivers have tended to be straightened and revetted in the interests of stable navigation and for the most rapid downstream transport of water. Such regulated environments lose species diversity and overall productivity as well as being aesthetically unappealing. Several steps are available for channel restoration for fish:

- improvement of in-channel diversity through installation of boulders, low weirs and deflectors;
- improvement of streamside cover though use of vegetation or artificial structures;
- reduction of slope of levees or confining embankments;
- reinstatement of pool-riffle sequences in low order streams;
- construction of shallow bays connected to main channel;
- set back levees to create multi-stage channels;
- remeander stream within confines of setback;
- creation of point bars, islands and gravel banks.

Each of these successive steps is aimed at increasing the diversity of the main channel. This produces a corresponding diversification of the fish as a greater range of shelter, breeding and feeding habitats become available for the different species and life stages. Apart from their value to fish a number of other environmental services are provided by rehabilitation of this type. It has been shown, for example, that the leakage of nutrients from agricultural activities in the catchment can be substantially reduced by the presence of a vegetated buffer strip along the riparian zone.

Restoration of Longitudinal Connectivity

One of the major problems with river regulation is the ease with which longitudinal migratory patterns can be disrupted. Even relatively low dams and weirs will form insurmountable barriers to non-salmonid species. The interruption of migratory pathways clearly impacts most severely on obligate migrants which have to move upstream or downstream to breed. It can also affect the stock structure of more static populations where genetic mixing is no longer possible and local stocks diminished by overfishing or disease can no longer be replenished from elsewhere in the system.

The most obvious method to improve fish passage over obstacles such as weirs and dams is to remove the structure. However this usually leaves a head of water to be dissipated which is often excessive for fish passage. Furthermore the high flows involved with large differences in water level accelerate erosion and affect lateral land through lowering of the water level. Four main approaches are adopted to allow fish to pass obstructions while at the same time avoiding these problems by lengthening the channel through which the head is dissipated. These are:

- fish slopes and rock ramps;
- pool and Denil type fishways;
- bypass channels and biocanals;
- fishlifts and locks.

Restoration of Lateral Connectivity

Separation of lateral floodplains from the main channel may occur through deliberate construction of bunds or levees for channel training for navigation, and land reclamation for agricultural or urban development. Isolation of the floodplain can also occur incidentally when flood pulses are diminished by dams constructed upstream and when the channel be is eroded in response to lessened silt loads. Restoration, particularly of limnophilic and phytophylic species in the river depends on the reconnection of the floodplain to the channel. Floodplain restoration projects of this type are relatively uncommon due to their extensive nature and to the costs involved. Essentially, however, most proposals call for the destruction of artificial river training structures such as levees. The full original extent of flooding can rarely be reintroduced particularly in very flat floodplains and here replacement levees will be required set back sufficiently far from the channel as to allow adequate flooding. Other approaches include the installation of submerged weirs across eroded channels, flood retention structures across the floodplain to divert water into abandoned channels and lagoons, and the incorporation of new features such as gravel pits into the system.

Implementation

States should ensure that an effective legal and administrative framework at the local and national level, as appropriate, is established for fisheries resource conservation and fisheries management.

States should ensure that laws and regulations provide for sanctions applicable in respect of violations which are adequate in severity to be effective, including sanctions which allow for the refusal, withdrawal or suspension of authorizations to fish in the event of non-compliance with conservation and management measures in force.

Whilst it is important to institute sanctions within the fishery sector to ensure adherence to agreed policies and agreements, the major impacts on the inland resource arise, as we have seen, from outside the fisheries sector. Because of this it is important that systems of sanctions exist that are of sufficient weight to ensure compliance of polluting and impacting users throughout the basin as a whole.

States, in conformity with their national laws, should implement effective fisheries monitoring, control, surveillance and law enforcement measures including, where appropriate, observer programmes, inspection schemes and vessel monitoring systems. Such measures should be promoted and, where appropriate, implemented by subregional or regional fisheries management organizations and arrangements in accordance with procedures agreed by such organizations or arrangements.

States and subregional or regional fisheries management organizations and arrangements, as appropriate, should agree on the means by which the activities of such organizations and arrangements will be financed, bearing in mind, inter alia, the relative benefits derived from the fishery and the differing capacities of countries to provide financial and other contributions. Where appropriate, and when possible, such organizations and arrangements should aim to recover the costs of fisheries conservation, management and research.

Support to river basin organizations: The provision of funding to river basin authorities to enable them to pursue a fisheries agenda is particularly important. Many of the other activities can be sufficiently financed by the comparatively rich sectors they represent whereas fisheries is insufficiently funded to ensure adequate representation. Because of this many attempts to incorporate fisheries into river basin commissions have failed.

States which are members of or participants in subregional or regional fisheries management organizations or arrangements should implement internationally agreed measures adopted in the framework of such organizations or arrangements and consistent with international law to deter the activities of vessels flying the flag of non-members or non-participants which engage in activities which undermine the effectiveness of conservation and management measures established by such organizations or arrangements.

Financial Institutions

Without prejudice to relevant international agreements, States should encourage banks and financial institutions not to require, as a condition of a loan or mortgage, fishing vessels or fishing support vessels to be flagged in a jurisdiction other than that of the State of beneficial ownership where such a requirement would have the effect of increasing the likelihood of non-compliance with international conservation and management measures.

Financing for inland fisheries: Inland fishers have often limited or no access to the formal credit market (banks) because of their lack of assets acceptable as collateral, and the small-scale and often remoteness of their operations. In these circumstances, they often need to rely exclusively on the financial services of middlemen who may face limited competition and can charge high interest rates. Governments should consider improving the access of inland fishers to the formal credit market through, for example, micro-credit schemes in line with the Grameen Bank concept of Bangladesh.

Funding other users of the aquatic resource: Funding may also be desirable to extend financial incentives for ecologically friendly behaviour by industry, agriculture, and other sectors in their use of inland aquatic resources. Subsidies for investment in waste treatment plants, fish ladders, etc. may be justified in certain situations where the strict application of the polluter-pays principle is impractical or, as may be the case in poor countries, may undermine the industry's competitiveness.

Fishery Management
Edited by: Dr. Rabi N. Misra
ISBN: 978-93-5056-789-0
Edition: 2016
Published by: Discovery Publishing House Pvt. Ltd., New Delhi (India)

Fishing Industry and Fisher Folk Existence through Micro-credit Services for India and Bangladesh

Dr. Rookesh Kumar Mishra
MMM, MBA, Ph.D.
Now Working as Senior H.R. Manager in New Delhi

Introduction

The Bay of Bengal is ever so illustrious for her magnificent fisheries resources in the world. Her territory generours fisheries resources including waters are uniquely endowed for bringing bonanza for her adjoining areas. As a contiguous country, Bangaldesh and India are well blessed by the highly diverse and enriched fisheries resources of the Bay of Bengal and hence coastal fisheries resource of Bangladesh and India are very flourishing and virtuously bountiful in this macrocosm. The term "Coastal fisheries sector" broadly refers to both artisanal fisheries (capture fishery) and coastal aquaculture (culture fishery) and hence commonly means the associated livelihood of fisherfolk, shrimp fry collector and coastal aquafarmers Despite the potential importance of microfinance as a tool for financial inclusion and for poverty alleviation, a surprisingly low proportion of financial policies in the Asia Pacific Region include specific reference to it. Evidence from evaluation studies of past initiatives suggests that formal credit programmes through cooperatives and rural banks, often supported by donor agencies, are often not successful, both in terms of the viability of lending institutions in outreach and the ability of intended beneficiaries to access cheaper sources of credit.

Informal savings schemes and credit markets are widely developed in many countries and may positively contribute to providing access to capital or assets because they are closer to the users, more flexible, have user friendly process and procedures and more adapted to the client's micro credit needs (BOBP, 2004).

An enormous variety of water bodies throughout Bangladesh and India considerable potential for fish production and cultivation, but a general lack of capital, access to resources and knowledge means that many farmers are unable to provide all the commercial inputs required for intensive production methods. Many NGOs are adopting strategies to minimise the inherent riskiness of fish culture by undertaking research into low-input systems, low-cost technology, fast growing species and alternative management practices. Few microfinance institutions or commercial banks exist that are willing and able to provide small loans to small-scale fisher people at interest rates much lower than through middlemen.

Fisher people also consider the perceived inflexibility of banks as a big disadvantage in timely access to finance, due to involved documentation and collateral based lending norms. Globally, women constitute the majority of microfinance clients, primarily because of their excellent loan repayment records and micro savings. They play an important role in fishing communities, encompassing social and economic responsibilities and duties, within and outside their households.

Women are particularly involved in productive activities directly related to fisheries production, processing and marketing as well as in non-fisheries income-generating activities. Loan size requirements are frequent but small, which makes them appropriate clients of microfinance. There is a demand for savings and credit services among the fisher people that is rarely met because they rarely have access to institutional finance. Microfinance is needed by the households to increase their income from fisheries activities and other income-generating activities. It is also required for social needs related to their quality of life and for smoothening consumption patterns, particularly during lean and off-seasons when little or no income or food is generated. Microfinance also helps in managing risks and reducing economic and social vulnerability.

Materials and Methods

The study was designed for an intensive review of the development of microfinance services for coastal small scale fisheries and aquaculture in Bangladesh and India with specific attention to women, based on a review of available literature, web-based materials and information, and the experience of organizations like National Bank for Agriculture and Rural Development (NABARD), connected with promotion and development of microfinance in the sector. Review of literature was conducted using searchable database. From the references on the subject, identified literature was gathered from libraries and internet sources and an assessment of the current scenario was made to prepare the background of the paper as well as to collect data pertaining to the objectives of the present study. A format for collection of information capturing the objectives and the issues concerning the review exercise was drawn up and the same was provided to the identified agencies for collecting the necessary data and information from the stakeholders involved in small scale fisheries and aquaculture development and extending finance/microfinance services. Analysis of the data and information was carried out for drawing inferences and finalization of recommendations.

Results and Discussion

The study of the fisheries sector in India and Bangladesh is a study in contrasts. In India, the major thrust is on the inland fisheries sector while the brackish water and marine sectors are basic export earners. In Bangladesh, there is a large artisanal and coastal fisheries sector and equally large inland fisheries sector. The conclusion is that fisheries play an important role in national economies of both the countries, providing full time or part time employment to a considerable proportion of the poorer people living in coastal areas. Most of the fisher people are not financially included and have little or no access to credit and insurance facilities. However, microfinance agencies or self help groups or fisher's associations have provided some financial inclusion services. Marine fish production from near shore waters has reached almost a plateau and, at best, only marginal increase is predicted from this zone. Major gap in total fishable potential and present production exists in deep sea and off shore pelagic resources. Good potential exists for coastal aquaculture and man-culture. Resource enhancement measures in coastal waters also need to be taken up. In contrast, inland fish production has been showing rapid growth of about 6% per annum and has great potential for further development. Area expansion, diversification of farmed species and augmenting productivity from the existing farms in a sustainable manner are possible strategies in this sector. A substantial portion of the future additional demand for fish will have to be met from aquaculture due to massive and unplanned depletion of marine fish stocks, worldwide. In the marine sector besides intensifying coastal aquaculture, sea farming, intensification of deep-sea fishing, better management of coastal fisheries with application of principles of sustainability and stock enhancement measures would be practiced for maximizing returns. Considering the massive processing facilities created and the skilled manpower available, import of raw material for processing, value addition and export has good prospects (FAO, 2009; Hossain et al, 2007) Marine fisheries sector of Bangladesh and India faces frequent fluctuations as cyclic and climatologically effects influence the pelagic stocks. All the coastal States in India have enacted their Marine Fishing Regulation Act with jurisdiction over their territorial waters. Management measures such as closed seasons, delimitation of fishing zones for different categories of fishing craft etc. are implemented for ensuring sustainability. Capture of non-targeted species and rejection of by catches are discouraged through awareness programmes involving stakeholders. Conservation of aquatic resources and genetic biodiversity is another thrust area for the next millennium. These two countries are party to the Convention on Biological Diversity and Bio safety protocol. Necessary safeguards are put in place for regulating cross-border movement of live aquatic organisms. Attention is paid to protect endangered marine species such as Olive Ridley turtles by declaring marine sanctuaries and no-fishing zones along their nesting sites. Turtle Excluder Devices have been made mandatory for trawlers in the vulnerable areas. Fishing for endangered species of fin fishes, crustaceans and molluscs listed under IUCN is banned and studies on the vulnerable species have been taken up. Apart from areas listed under Ramsar sites, other ecological hotspots are identified for abetting pollution and restoration of fisheries etc fighting land-based pollution and implementation of Integrated Coastal Zone Management has high priority (FAO, 2009).

Besides its active involvement in the fisheries developmental initiatives of FAO's COFI and its subcommittees, both the countries are associated with various other global and regional bodies dealing with fisheries such as Convention for Conservation of Antarctic Marine Living Resources (CCMLR), Commission for International Trade on Endangered Species (CITES), International Whaling Commission (IWC), Indo-Pacific Fisheries Commission (IPFC), Indian Ocean Tuna Commission (IOTC). Among the regional fisheries management initiatives, India hosts the eight-member Bay of Bengal Large Marine Ecosystem (BOBLME) programme in Chennai, the first phase of which has been completed. Another four country regional initiative, namely the Bay of Bengal Programme - Inter-governmental Organization (BOBP-IGO) is also hosted by India and is situated in Chennai. Fisheries issues are also actively debated in other regional fora such as SAARC, BIMSTEC-EC,

IOR-RC etc. in which the South Asian countries are members. There are a number of bilateral assistance programmes for development of fisheries. FAO UNDP Bay of Bengal Programme (BOBP), a regional initiative covering seven countries bordering the Bay of Bengal started in 1979 was concluded during 2003. Assistance was received under the Program in the development of small-scale fisheries, including enhancing the socioeconomic conditions of the fishing communities in the region. ODA UK provided technical aid for prevention of post-harvest losses in marine fisheries. The processing sector has largely benefited from the FAO programme for technical assistance in implementing HACCP in seafood processing industries, NORAD assistance for developing deep sea fisheries and cold water fisheries, DANIDA assistance in coastal fisheries development and manpower training in marine fisheries, Japanese assistance in development of deep sea fishing, acquisition of modern dredging equipment, manpower training and capacity addition in net making and French assistance in fresh water prawn farming has helped development of these sub sectors.

Presently an FAO assisted programme for controlling shrimp disease is under implementation in Andhra Pradesh. A programme for developing cleaner fishing harbours with FAO assistance is under finalization. The information and data pertaining to micro finance in fisheries sector and consequently small scale fisheries and aquaculture sector in all the three countries is not readily available. As the mandate of the present exercise is to prepare a review paper on microfinance in the coastal small scale fisheries and aquaculture sector, there is little scope of conducting any field study to generate the necessary data in this regard. In the absence of published data on microfinance in this context, the following procedure has been adopted to make an assessment of the flow of micro finance to the sector. Data submitted to Micro Finance Information Exchange (MIX), a web based micro finance gateway has been relied upon. The data for two consecutive years i.e. for 2007 and 2008 have been generated for the respective countries i.e.

Bangladesh and India using the database The database does not offer sectoral data. An effort has been made to assess the sectoral credit flow through micro finance route by following two independent methods i.e. (*i*) following the ratio of fisheries GDP to the total GDP of the country and working out the share of micro credit of the small scale coastal fisheries & aquaculture in that ratio of the respective countries and (*ii*) working out the share of micro credit to fishermen to the total micro credit disbursement of each country in the ratio of fishermen population to total population of the respective country The lower of the two assessments following the two methods have been considered for the present assessment of micro credit flow to the sector. The microfinance flow in the coastal fisheries sector of India and Bangladesh is estimated to be US $ 12.81 million and 6.39 million respectively. There is considerable scope for increasing microcredit to this sector, if low cost funds are available. The data on bank finance to fisheries sector in case of Bangladesh was not readily available. The available data on flow of credit through regular banking channel to the fisheries sector was analysed for the coastal states of India. There is no clear trend in GLC flow in the sector through regular banking channel comprising the scheduled Commercial Banks, Regional Rural Banks, Co-operative Banks. The credit flow to the sector in coastal districts through regular bank finance has been in the range of INR 9633 to 10392. The agency wise share of microfinance to total credit flow to the sector in the coastal States was analyzed which reflects the share of regular banking channel to be 94.41%. The balance credit flow is through the microfinance route comprising of SHG-BLP accounting for 4.02% and MFIs accounting for 1.57% (Khandker, 1998) In the absence of readily available data on credit need of the coastal marine fisheries and aquaculture sector of the Bangladesh and India, an assessment has been made in respect of India utilizing available data on occupation profile of coastal fishermen in India.

Marine Fisheries

The credit need for replacement of the existing units @ 15% per annum have been considered. The bank loan component has been worked out considering margin money to be 25% for mechanized fishing units, 15% for the motorized fishing units and 10% for the non mechanized units. In India, the financial services gap is high considering the fact that apart from South Indian Federation of Fishermen Society (SIFFS), DHAN Foundation, there is no other player which provides any kind of insurance products. The social intermediation, enterprise development and social services are provided under the SHG-BLP and by MFIs. The coverage is not uniform and are largely concentrated in the pockets covered by SIFFS, Dhan Foundation, Matsyafed, Church organizations, ICNW, etc. However, Bangladesh Grameen Bank, ASA, Community Development and Empowerment Community (CODEC), Bangladesh Rural Advancement Council (BRAC), Bangladesh Rural Development Board (BRDB), Darido Bimochon Foundation (PDBF) offer comprehensive services covering all possible intermediation comprising of financial, social and enterprise development services (Khandker, 1998).

According to a United Nation's report, women perform 65% of the world's work, receive only 10% of the world's income and own only 1% of the total assets. Though the transformation of fisheries sector due to mechanization, has enabled multi-faceted changes in the role and contribution of fisherwomen, the overall structural changes in the marine fisheries sector brought about by extensive use of ice in local markets and export-oriented development efforts have dislodged a large proportion of women from employment sectors like fish drying, curing, dry fish trade and net making. Human dependence on marine and coastal resources is increasing day by day. Today, small scale fisheries employ 50 milllion of the world's 51 million fishers, practically all of whom are from developing countries. And together they produce more than half of the world's annual marine fish catch of 98 millions tones, supplying most of the fish consumed in the developing world. There are about 0.5 million fisher households located all along the Indian coast and a total of 3 million fisher folk inhabiting the coastal villages. The average number of sea going fishermen is 282 in a coastal village.

Out of the 1.2 million fisher folk in post harvest sector, women occupy a considerable proportion of more than 0.5 million (FAO, 2007). On the other hand, coastal fisheries resource of Bangladesh serves as the only primary source of income and nutrition of over 484,000 household and 2.7 million family members. According to the coastal zone policy of the Government of Bangladesh, 19 districts out of 64 are in the coastal zone covering a total of 147 upazillas. Total population living in the coastal zone is 35.1 million that represent 28 percent of total population of the country. The average number of sea going fishermen is 150 in a coastal village. Out of the 1 million fisher folk in post harvest sector, women occupy a considerable proportion of more than 0.2 million (PDO-ICZMP, 2003; Chowdhury 2008).

They play a significant role in the pre and post harvest operations in capture fisheries while their presence is conspicuous in all the stages of culture fisheries. Their role in household management is far higher than that of women of other sectors. Majority of the labour force in the pre-processing and processing plants of shrimp are women. Women also contribute a major proportion of the workforce in export-oriented processing of cuttlefish, lobsters and finfish varieties. In the fishers' community women either like taking the roles of a housewife or go for some income generating occupation. In a traditional fisheries society, a woman's social status is often referred with respect to that of her husband. When a fisherwoman goes for some job, it will be mostly counted as the inability of her husband to support the family. Because of the same reason the women usually do not enjoy the freedom to go for some work or interact with change agents, especially when the agents are males. Nevertheless, few exceptions are there who overcome the barriers of society in the struggle for existence and they, in due course, develop behavioral modification, characteristic of androgyny (FAO, 2007).

Fisherwomen in any work sector can be found occupying the position of a sub category or performing supportive roles.

At landing centres women engaged in fish drying collect small sized by-catches. In markets women usually sell low value products in a remote comer. Though highly nutritive and helping to meet the nutritive demands of these by-catches fetch very low price and a poor profit margin for the women. Wholesalers among women are very few, like at markets in Trivandrum and Mangalore.

Perception of Fisherwomen towards Various Economic Issues

(1) Lack of secure marketing channel (2) Poor income (3) Inadequate saving schemes (4) Lack of marketing information (5) Poor working capital (*Source*: The author's survey, 2010) Lack of alternate employment in off-seasons leads to forced borrowing from money lenders at very high interest rate of 10 per cent month or even more. Though they work hard in peak season, they can hardly pay back the money, as it would have doubled by then. The vicious circle of indebtedness continues. Women in value addition sector also sell their products to local petty shops and households. The inadequate information support on markets and lack of sound distribution networks are reasons behind this. The problem is not the lack of opportunities but is of unawareness about these opportunities (FAO, 2007).

Conclusion

Empowerment of the individuals, both male and female members should be assured which gains significance in the context of ever changing technological options in marine fisheries. There are many areas in capture fisheries sector with ample scope for employing fisherwomen. Several mariculture technologies ensure enough scope for accommodating women in large numbers. More effort is to be put towards filling the gaps in program planning rather than program implementation. Researchers also have to pay sufficient attention for identifying the needs of fisherwomen and thereby generating women-friendly technologies. Women empowerment and thereby the community development through combined efforts of men and womenfolk requires a holistic approach.

The studies conducted have observed the following activities of Women in Fisheries in India and Bangladesh are: (1) Clam collection, (2) Sorting, (3) Marketing, (4) Fresh fish marketing, (5) Dressing of fish (Surumi Units), (6) Aquaculrure (Fish farms, Shrimp farms and shrimp hatcheries), (7) Processing plants (Peelers, Graders, Packers), (8) Labour at Landing centres (Loading ice to boat, unloading fish from boat, loading fish to tempos, sorting of fish), (9) Traditional fish processing (Salting and drying offish) and (10) By product units (Fish meal, fish oil, liver oil units and Manure).

During the investigation following constraints have been found for development of Fisher women and such kinds of problems are: (1) Limited access to resources, (2) Lack of access to leadership positions and voice in decision making, (3) Inadequate training and formal education, (4) High disparity in ownership of productive assets and wage structure, (5) Exploitation by middlemen and contractors, (6) Intensive labour and long working hours, (7) Lack of interest in occupations other than fisheries, (8) Lack of credit facilities, (9) Socio-economic frame work with traditional customs and conventions, (10) Inadequate health care for occupational hazards and (11) Lack of knowledge in latest technologies of aquaculrure and post harvest management.

The sustainable development of the coastal fisheries and aquaculrure sector is yet another major challenge. The over capacity and over exploitation in the sector is a glaring feature, globally. Use of destructive and wasteful fishing methods like trawling and purse seining and their impact on coastal resources, is a matter of concern. Use of beach seines and gears of small mesh size in artisanal marine fisheries sector is also a potential threat to sustainable development. Implementation of FAO's code of responsible fishing and retirement of vessels in sectors where excess capacity has been created, needs to be supported strongly by the development agencies and the financial institutions.

REFERENCES

BOBP, 2004. Poverty alleviation in small scale fishing communities. 4(1) : 6-10

Chowdhury, M.S.N. Hossain, M.S. & Barua, P. (2008). Artisanal Fisheries Status, and Sustainable Management Options in Teknaf Coast, Bangladesh.

Chowdhury, M.S.N., Hossain, M.S., Das, N.G., & Barua, P. 2011. Environmental variables and fisheries diversity of the Naaf River Estuary, Bangladesh. Journal of Coastal Conservation.

Hossain, M.S., Das, N. G. & Chowdhury, M.S.N. (2007). Fisheries Management of the Naaf River. Chittagong, Coastal and Ocean Research Group of Bangladesh, 257 pp.

Khandker, S. 1998. Fighting Poverty with micro credits (Oxford University Press, Oxford). Washington, D. C : World Bank KHANDKER, S. 2005. Microfinance and Poverty: Evidence using panel data from Bangladesh. World Bank Economic Review, 19. 262-286.

NABARD 2008. Status of microfinance in India published by Micro Credit Innovations Department, NABARD, India.

PDO-ICZMP, 2003. Coastal livelihoods and introductory analysis.

Program Development Office for the Integrated Coastal Zone Management Plan Project; working Paper WP011. Water Resources planning Organization; Ministry of Water Resources, Bangladesh.

Uwe Tietze and Lolita V Villareal. FAO Fisheries Technical Paper No. 440. Rome. FAO. 2007 Livelihood and micro enterprise development opportunities for women in coastal fishing communities in India - Case studies of Orissa and Maharashtra.

Fishery Management
Edited by: Dr. Rabi N. Misra
ISBN: 978-93-5056-789-0
Edition: 2016
Published by: Discovery Publishing House Pvt. Ltd.,
New Delhi (India)

CHAPTER 13

Fishery Management in India

Manoj Kumar Behera
Marketing Officer

Dr. Rabi Narayan Misra
Prof. MBA, Biju Patnaik University of Technology,
SMIT, Berhampur, Odisha

Introduction

From pre-historic period fishes have been used as protein-rich diet for human beings. The popularity of fishes has been mentioned in our religious literature like the *Ramayana* and the *Mahabharata*. In West Bengal, Bihar and Odisha the fish industry is about 1500 years old. In Bengal every family has at least one pond for fish. It is a blind belief that if Labeo rohita fish in particular is offered during the *Sradha* ceremony, the dead person will certainly go to heaven. There is also another view that human race originated near the water reservoir and the fishes provide valuable source of food supply to the inhabitants of the countries location in tropical regions.

In America the fishes of great lakes have considerable economics importance. Flesh of fish is a highly perishable commodity and the composition constitutes 60-80 per cent of water, 13-20 per cent of protein and greater or lesser amount of fat. The fish also contains phosphorus and Vitamins.

A fishery, including aquaculture provides an important source of protein food, employment, trade and economic well-being for the present and the future generation.

The wealth of aquatics resources was assumed to be an unlimited gift of nature. With increased knowledge and dynamic development fisheries after the World War II the myth has faded. It is realized that aquatic resources, although renewable and exhaustible are not infinite and thus need to be able to support the ever-increasing population is relativity becoming Paradoxical as 'Malthusian Pessimism' prevails in many parts of the world. In the context of rapid growing human population and increasing protein malnutrition, food security assumes greater signification in the developing countries.

The problem of 'protein gap' at present is more acute. The shortage of conventional food aggravates the problem. Producing more seafood from the sea can fill up the protein deficiency. The fish available in large quantities in the oceans would be able to meet the nutrition requirement of the mankind.

History of Fisheries

Fisheries and agriculture farming have evolved simultaneously in the history of human civilization. Interest in fish eating dates back to the dawn of history. It is believed that hunting for fish was not uncommon in pre-historic times. Near a river or lake or cave dwelling of the old stone age (4000 BC) heaps of shell fish and sea fish have been found. The great distance by which these sites were separation from the sea points out some primitive way of fish preservation like sun-drying and smoke-drying over the wood fire. It was practiced by these ancient dwellers to keep the food in edible condition. New Stone Age (10,000 BC) has also given evidence of salmon smoking practices. Bronze Age (3500 BC) was the time when salting offish starting. Trading in dried fish, of course,was in vogue with ancient civilization of Egypt, Mesopotamia and Indus valley. Many cities were christened according to their fishery activityviz. *Sidon* (meaning fishermen's town and *Malaga* (meaning the salting town) in the

Mediterranean. Among the Greeks and the Romans, fish became an important food of the rich and the poor. Iron Age (1000 BC) saw the great trades in dried, smoked and salted fish in Greece. It was during 400 BC to AD 450 a highly organized fishery emerged in the Roman Empire. In the middle age (AD 500 to AD 1500), fishmg activity was more pronounced in the Atlantic and gained importance. The empirical finding of the preservation methods like salting, drying smoking and poking in vinegar of the medieval times have come down to the present time. It was not until the beginning of the 18th century that preservation in ice in preserving the fish during transport. Ice preservation offish was introduced in England in 1786. Nineteenth century brought the time of scientific consideration. Application of science in agriculture by the middle of the 19th century led to agriculture outpacing the fishery industry. However, the application of science in fishing,deepsea fishing and fish culture hold enormous promise. The interest in the nutritive value scarcity in the Post World War I. In twenties and thirties the discovery of Vitamin A and D placed fish in prominent as it is rich in vitamin.

SOCIO-ECONOMIC PROFILE OF FISHERMEN

The Fishery Resources

The fishery resources are broadly divided into two classes. (*i*) Inland fisheries, and (*ii*) Marine fisheries

(*i*) Inland fisheries: The inland fisheries are a heterogeneous class, which covers culture fisheries that is fishing in ponds, nature and artificial lakes, swamps, rivers and canals. Apart from these fishing in coastal lagoon, estuaries and creeks has now become a part of inland fisheries, as both brackish water and fresh water aquaculture are including in this class. India is rank second in the world in inland fish production. A glimpse of India's diversified inland resources in Table 13.1.

Table 13.2 provides a glimpse of inland fishery resources of India. It shows rivers, mangroves, estuaries, reserves and upland lakes.

Table 13.1 : Fishery Resources of India

Resources	Resources Size
River (km)	29,000
Mangroves (ha)	3,56,000
Estuaries (ha)	3,00,000
Estuarine wetland (ha)	39,000
Backwater/Lagoon (ha)	1,90,500
Large and mediam reservation (ha)	16,67,809
Small reservoir (ha)	4,485,557
Flood Plan Wetland (ha)	2,02,313
Upland Lakes (ha)	7,20,000

***(ii)* Marine Fisheries:** This is wholly a capture-oriented sector and is largely exploited by marine fishermen through traditional and mechanized crafts and gears.

More than 70 percent of the fish landing in India are from the West coast and the rest from the East coast. The marine fishery resources are broadly divided into (1) Demersal and (2) Pelagic resources including Sharks and Rays; Eels, Perches, red mullets, Polynemid, Scianeids. Crustaceans, which are shellfish like prawn, non-penaeid prawn, lobsters, crabs, etc. have included in demersal resources, anise are 500 m depth and taken together their maximum sustainable yield is 84,000 metric tonnes per year.

The pelagic resources are usually telubed with the mid-water resources and it include oil, sardines, Hilsa, Ilisha, Clupeids, Flyingfish, Mackeral, Tunnies, Catfis,

Achavilla, Bombay, Duck, Ribbon fish mugil, Saurees, Pomprets and other Cephalopod. These resources can be exploited lower to 100 metres depth zone and their maximum sustainable yield is 40,800 metric tonnes per year (Lawson, 1984).

The marine fishing sectors in all the coastal States of India can be divided into three sub-sectors. These are as follows:

1. **Traditional sector:** It involves off-shore fishing operation with non-mechanised boats and traditional gears and operates within the 16 km to 20 km range from the coastline.
2. **Modern sector:** This sector with its small mechanized crafts and traditional craft operate within the mid sea, area within the 200 km range from the shore.
3. **Ultra-modern sector:** This sector with its large vessels namely deep-sea trawlers operate inthe deep-sea zone and beyond the operational area of the former two sub-sectors.

Indian Exclusive Economic Zone

The 2.02 million square km water so reads in an area of the Exclusive Economic Zone. In India, it extends up to 200 nautical miles with 8,085 km of coastline of the country from west to east around the peninsular India. The maritime States are Gujurat, Maharashtra, Goa, Karnataka, Kerala, Tamil Nadu, Lakshadweep, Puducherry, Andhra Pradesh, Odisha, West Bengal and Andaman and Nicobar Islands. It is illustrated in Table 13.2.

Table 13.2 : Potential of Fishhery Resourses in the Indian Exclusive Economic Zone

Depth Range(m)	0-50	50-200	200-500	Oceanic	Total
Demersal	1.28	0.625	0.03	0.00	1.933
Neretic Pelagic	1.00	0.74	0.00	0.00	1.74
Oceanic Pelagic	0.00	0.00	0.00	0.25	0.246
Total	2.28	1.369	0.028	0.246	3.921
Percentage	58.1	34.9	0.07	6.3	100

Table 13.2 shows total depth range relating to demersal. Neretic Pelagic, and oceanic pelagic and also shows total and percentage of catch.

Bio-geographical Zones

Fishing is generally limited to 11 to 16 km wide coastal waters having a total continental shelfarea of 2,59,000 sq. km along the 5650 km long coastline. Twelve biogeographical zones are distinguished along the coastline. They are:

- Kerela and South Malabar
- Malabar and South Kenara
- Konkan
- Mumbai and Gujurat
- Kathiawar
- Palk bay and Gulf of Mannar
- Coromandal North
- Coromandal South
- Andhra South
- Andhra Middle
- Andhra North
- West Bengal and Odisha

Important fishing areas on the west coast including: Gujarat Areas, Kankan area, North Canara area, South Canara area, and Malabar area.

Table 13.3 shows that among all the maritime States of India, Gujarat plays the first position followed by Andhra Prasdesh, Tamil Nadu, Kerela, Maharashtra and West Bengal. But now-a-days the maximum contribution of capture fishes are 60-70 per cent by mechanized boats and 25-30 per cent by traditional boats. The present level of exploitation of marine resources is about 75 per cent of the estimated potential of the EEZ. It was only 60 per cent in 1995-96. About 60-70 per cent of the marine catch comes from west coast and 25-35 per cent from east-coast and about 5 per cent from the islands. Pelagic fishes contribution about 35-45 per cent. Crustaceans contributes 15-20 perscent. Moluscans includes chank fisheries in the range of 5-15 percent.

North-west Coast

North west coast comprises Gujarat and Maharashtra, which contributes about 5-8 lakh tonnes of marine catch. The demersal fishes dominant with more than 60 per cent of the catch. Since the continental shelf is the most important species of demersal group of fishes are scianid, sharks, ray, cat fishes. Among the pelagic fishes clupeids like Hilsa is dominated while ribbon fishes contributed subsequently in the crustaceans groups. The non-penaeids, are most important while penaeids are landed in significant quantity.

Table 13.3 : Maritime States, Coast Line and Continental Shelf

Sl. No.	State/UTs	Coast line (km)	Coast line (%)	Continental shelf (sq. km)	Conti-nental shelf (%)
1.	Gujarat	1500	26. 5	120000	27. 4
2.	A. P	980	17. 3	39109	7. 9
3.	Tamil Nadu & Puducherry	960	17	34820+2488	8.5
4.	West Bengal & Odisha	200+480=680	12	7094+120166	8.5
5.	Maharashtra	600	10.6	—	—
6.	Kerela	560	9.9	38073	8.8
7.	Karnataka	270	4.8	24999	5.7
8.	Goa	110	1.9		
9.	A & N	—	—	34965	1.8
	Lakshadweep	—	—	7770	—

Source: Text Book of Fishery Science and Indian Fisheries, p. 34.

Major Markets

European Union continued to be the largest market for Indian marine products during the year 2005-06 also. Its share was 26.72 per cent in quantity 29.46 per cent in value, and 29.44 per cent in US$ realization. lt has registered an export growth of 16.22 per cent, 17.31 per cent and 19.39 per cent in quantity, value and US$ realization. The USA,the second largest market in term of value had a share of 10.90 per cent, 22.63 per cent and 22.98 per cent in quantity. It recorded a growth of 11.53 per cent in quantity, 5.34 per cent in value and 7.84 per cent in UV$ terms.

The share of Japan to our export market was 11.67 per cent in quantity, 15.96 per cent invalue, and 15.98 per cent in UV$. Export to Japan had shown a negative growth during the year 2005-06 by 3.87 per cent in value and 1.56 per cent in UV$ realization. However, Export to Middle East countries showed a tremendours growth by 33.96 per cent in quantity, 25.87 per cent in value and 27.30 per cent in UV$ terms. Export to China showed a marginal increaseof 9.81 per cent, 22.53 per cent and 27.30 per cent in quantity, value and US$.

Export to Canada, Tunisa, Puertorico, Russia, Lithuania, Reunion, Fuji Island, Bangladesh etc. showed a positive growth, whereas export to Mexico, Cyprus, Australia, Maldives Islands etc. showed a negative trend.

Conclusion

From pre-historic period fishes have been used as protein rich diet by human beings, India is the seventh largest fish producer in the world covering an area of 3. 29 million square km. Fishing is boardly classified into inland fisheries and marine fisheries. Inland fisheries cover rivers, mangroves, estuaries, backwater, lagoon, etc. India occupies second position in inland fish production of the world. Marine fishery is wholly a caputure oriented sector. India has a coast of 8085 km. having 3638 fishing villages. India occupies tenth position in total fish production of the world. Marine fishery resouces are boardly divided into two types : Demersal and Pelagic. In India there are twelve bio-geographic zones. Inland capture fishery contributes at least 30 per cent of the total fish production.

Marine fishery help to earn foreign exchange for the country. There is a steady increase of foreign exchange. In the year 2004-05 India earned ₹ 7245.30 crores by exporting fish to other countries. The chief importing countries are Japan, USA, European Union, China, India also export marine products to these countries. The Ports used for export of marine product are Chennai, Kochi, Kolkata, etc.

REFERENCES

Agrawal S.C. *Fishery Management*, Ashish Publishing House, New Delhi.

Anderson. L. G. *Economic Impacts of Externded Fisheries Jurisdiction*, Ann Arbor Science Publishers, Michigan.

Bhattaacharya, S.N. *Fisheries in Indian Economic*, Delhi Book Publishers, Delhi.

Bichwal, N. "Trends in Marine Fishery Production In India", Bombay Book Publication House, Bombay.

Brandt, A. V. Fish catching methods of the World" *Fishing*, New Books Publishers Ltd., London.

Badapanda, H.S. "Studies on chilika Lake"; *Milestones*, Published in *Fishish Chimes*, Vol. 18, Chimes House, Visakhapamam, Andhra Pradesh.

Bal, D. V. and Rao, V. K. *Marine Fisheries of India*, Tata McGraw-Hill Publishising Company Ltd, New Delhi.

Christy, F. T and Scoot, A. D. *The Common Wealth in Ocean Fisheries*, John Hopkins Press, Baltimore.

Dhar, P. K., *Hidian Economy*: its *Growing Dimension*, Kalyani Publications, Cuttack.

Fishery Management
Edited by: **Dr. Rabi N. Misra**
ISBN: 978-93-5056-789-0
Edition: **2016**
Published by: **Discovery Publishing House Pvt. Ltd., New Delhi (India)**

Sustainability of Fisheries

Dr. P. Shanumukha Rao
Lecturer in Commerce,
Government College (A), Rajahmundry, A.P.

Fisheries have rarely been 'sustainable'. Rather, fishing has induced serial depletions, long masked by improved technology, geographic expansion and exploitation of previously spurned species lower in the food web. With global catches declining since the late 1980s, continuation of present trends will lead to supply shortfall, for which aquaculture cannot be expected to compensate, and may well exacerbate. Reducing fishing capacity to appropriate levels will require strong reductions of subsidies. Zoning the oceans into unfished marine reserves and areas with limited levels of fishing effort would allow sustainable fisheries, based on resources embedded in functional, diverse ecosystems.

Fishing is the catching of aquatic wildlife, the equivalent of hunting bison, deer and rabbits on land. Thus, it is not surprising that industrial-scale fishing should generally not be sustainable: industrial-scale hunting, on land, would not be, either. What is surprising rather, is how entrenched the notion is that unspecified 'environmental change' caused, and continues to cause, the collapse of exploited fish populations. Examining the history of fishing and fisheries makes it abundantly clear that humans have had for thousands of years a major impact on target species and their supporting ecosystems. Indeed, the archaeological literature contains many examples of ancient human fishing associated with gradual shifts, through time, to smaller sizes and the serial depletion of species that we now recognize as the symptoms of overfishing.

This literature supports the claim that, historically, fisheries have tended to be non-sustainable, although not unexpectedly there is a debate about the cause for this, and the exceptions-. The few uncontested historical examples of sustainable fisheries seem to occur where a superabundance of fish supported small human populations in challenging climates. Sustainability occurred where fish populations were naturally protected by having a large part of their distribution outside of the range of fishing operations. Hence, many large old fecund females, which contribute overwhelmingly to the egg production that renews fish populations, remained untouched. How important such females can be is illustrated by the example of a single ripe female red snapper, *Lutjanus campechanus,* of 61 cm and 12. 5 kg, which contains the same number of eggs (9,300,000) as 212 females of 42 cm and 1.1 kg each. Where such natural protection was absent, that is, where the entire population was accessible to fishing gears, depletion ensued, even if the gear used seems inefficient in retrospec. This was usually masked, however, by the availability of other species to target, leading to early instances of depletions observable in the changing size and species composition of fish remains, for example, in middens.

The fishing process became industrialized in the early nineteenth century when English fishers started operating steam trawlers, soon rendered more effective by power winches and, after the First World War, diesel engines. The aftermath of the Second World War added another 'peace dividend' to the industrialization of fishing: freezer trawlers, radar and acoustic fish finders. The fleets of the Northern Hemisphere were ready to take on the world.

Fisheries science advanced over this time as well: the two world wars had shown that strongly exploited fish populations, such as those of the North Sea, would recover most, if not all, of their previous abundance when released from fishing. This allowed the construction of models of single-species fish populations whose size is affected only by fishing pressure, expressed either as a fishing mortality rate (*F*, or catch/biomass ratio), or by a measure of fishing effort (*f*, for example, trawling hours per year) related to *F* through a catchability coefficient (*q*): $F = qf$. Here, *q* represents the fraction of a population caught by one unit of effort, directly expressing the effectiveness of a gear. Thus, *q* should be monitored as closely as fishing effort itself, if the impact of fishing on a given stock, as expressed by *F*, is to be evaluated. Technology changes tend to increase *q*, leading to increases referred to as 'technology coefficient', which quickly renders meaningless any attempts to limit fishing mortality by limiting only fishing effort.

Fisheries go Global

In 1950, the newly founded Food and Agriculture Organization (FAO) of the United Nations began collection of global statistics. Fisheries in the early 1950s were at the onset of a period of extremely rapid growth, both in the Northern Hemisphere and along the coast of the countries of what is now known as the developing world. Everywhere that industrial-scale fishing (mainly trawling, but also purse seining and long-lining) was introduced, it competed with small-scale, or artisanal fisheries. This is especially true for tropical shallow waters (10-100 m), where artisanal fisheries targeting food fish for local consumption, and trawlers targeting shrimps for export, and discarding the associated by-catch, compete for the same resource. Throughout the 1950s and 1960s, this huge increase of global fishing effort led to an increase in catches) so rapid that their trend exceeded human population growth, encouraging an entire generation of managers and politicians to believe that launching more boats would automatically lead to higher catches.

Estimated Global Fish Landings

Figures for invertebrates, groundfish, pelagic fish and *Peruvian anchoveta* are from FAO catch statistics, with adjustment for over-reporting from China. Fish caught but then discarded were not included in the FAO landings; data relate to the early 1990s were made proportional to the FAO landings for other periods. Other illegal, unreported or unregulated (IUU) catches were estimated by identifying, for each 5-year block, the dominant jurisdiction and gear use (and hence incentive for IUU); reported catches were then raised by the percentage of IUU in major fisheries for each 5-year block. The resulting estimates of IUU are very tentative (note dotted *y*-axis), and we consider that complementing landings statistics with more reliable estimates of discards and IUU is crucial for a transition to ecosystem-based management.

The first collapse with global repercussions was that of the *Peruvian anchoveta* in 1971-1972, which is often perceived as having been caused by an El Nino event. However, much of the available evidence, including actual catches (about 18 million tonnes) exceeding officially reported catches (12 million tonnes), suggest that overfishing was implicated as well. But attributing the collapse of the *Peruvian anchoveta* to 'environmental effects' allowed business as usual to continue and, in the mid-1970s, this led to the beginning of a decline in total catches from the North Atlantic. The declining trend accelerated in the late 1980s and early 1990s when most of the cod stocks off New England and eastern Canada collapsed, ending fishing traditions reaching back for centuries.

Despite these collapses, the global expansion of effort continued and trade in fish products intensified to the extent that they have now become some of the most globalized commodities, whose price increased much faster than the cost of living index. In 1996, FAO published a chronicle of global fisheries showing that a rapidly increasing fraction of world catches originate from stocks that are depleted or collapsed, that is, 'senescent' in FAO's parlance. Yet, global catches seemed to continue, increasing through the 1990s according to official catch statistics. This surprising result was explained recently when massive over-reporting of marine fisheries catches by one single country, the People's Republic of China, was uncovered. Correcting for this showed that reported world fisheries landings have in fact been declining slowly since the late 1980s, by about 0.7 million tonnes per year.

Fisheries Impact on Ecosystem and Biodiversity

The position within ecosystems of the fishes and invertebrates landed by fisheries can be expressed by their trophic levels, expressing the number of steps they are removed from the algae (occupying a trophic level of 1) that fuel marine food web. Most food fishes have trophic levels ranging from 3.0 to 4.5, that is, from sardines feeding on zooplankton to large cod or tuna feeding on miscellaneous fishes. Thus, the observed global decline of 0.05-0.10 trophic levels per decade in global fisheries landings is extremely worrisome, as it implies the gradual removal of large, long-lived fishes from the ecosystems of the world oceans. This is perhaps most clearly illustrated by a recent study in the North Atlantic showing that the biomass of predatory fishes (with a trophic level of 3.75 or more) declined by two-thirds through the second half to the twentieth century, even though this area was already severely depleted before the start of this time period.

Fisheries, Both Marine and Freshwater, are Characterized by a Decline of the Mean Trophic Level in the Landings, Implying an Increased Reliance on Organisms Low in Food Webs.

Freshwater fisheries have lower trophic level values overall, indicating an earlier onset of the 'fishing down' phenomenon. The trend is inverted in non-Asian aquaculture, whose production consists increasingly of piscivorous organisms, as

Norway (a major producer, yet representative country).

It may be argued that so-called 'fishing down marine food webs' is both a good and an unavoidable thing, given a growing demand for fish. Indeed, the initial ecosystem reaction to the process may be a release from predation, where cascading effects may lead to increased catches. Such effects are, however, seldom observed in marine ecosystems, mainly because they do not function simply as a number of unconnected food chains. Rather, predators operate within finely meshed food webs, whose structure (which they help maintain) tends to support the production of their prey. Hence, the concept of 'beneficial predation', where a predator may have a direct negative impact on its prey, but also an indirect positive effect, by consuming other predators and competitors of the prey. Thus, removing predators does not necessarily lead to more of their prey becoming available for humans. Instead, it leads to increases or outbursts of previously suppressed species, often invertebrates, some of which may be exploited (for example, squid or jellyfish, the latter a relatively new resource, exported to east Asia), and some outright noxious.

The principal, direct impact of fishing is that it reduces the abundance of target species. It has often been assumed that this does not impose any direct threat of species extinction as marine fish generally are very fecund and the ocean expanse is wide. But the past few decades have witnessed a growing awareness that fishes can not only be severely depleted, but also be threatened with extinction through overexploitation. Among commercially important species, those particularly at risk are species that are highly valued, large and slow to mature, have limited geographical range, and/or have sporadic recruitment. There is actually little support, though, for the general assumption that the most highly fecund marine fish species are less susceptible to overexploitation; rather it seems that this perception is flawed. Fisheries may also change the evolutionary characteristics of populations by selectively removing the larger, fast-growing individuals, and one important research question is whether this induces irreversible changes in the gene pool. Overall, this has implications for research, monitoring and management, and it points to the need for incorporating ecological consideration in fisheries management, as exemplified by the development of quantitative guidelines to avoid local extinctions.

Another worrisome aspect of fishing down marine food webs is that it involves a reduction of the number and length of pathways linking food fishes to the primary producers, and hence a simplification of the food webs. Diversified food webs allow predators to switch between prey as their abundance fluctuates, and hence to compensate for prey fluctuations induced by environmental fluctuations. Fisheries-induced food-web simplification, combined with the drastic fisheries-induced reduction in the number of year classes in predator populations, makes their reduced biomass strongly dependent of annual recruitment. This leads to increasing variability, and to lack of predictability in population sizes, and hence in predicted catches. The net effect is that it will increasingly look like environmental fluctuations impact strongly on fisheries resources, even where they originally did not. This resolves, if in a perverse way, the question of the relative importance of fisheries and environmental variability as the major driver for changes in the abundance of fisheries resources.

It seems unbelievable in retrospect, but there was a time when it was believed that bottom trawling had little detrimental impact, or even a beneficial impact, on the sea bottom that it 'ploughed'. Recent research shows that the ploughing analogy is inappropriate and that if an analogy is required, it should be that of clear cutting forests in the course of hunting deer. Indeed, the productivity of the benthic organisms at the base of food webs leading to food fishes is seriously impacted by bottom trawling, as is the survival of their juveniles when deprived of the biogenic bottom structure destroyed by that form of fishing. Hence, given the extensive coverage of the world's shelf ecosystems by bottom trawling, it is not surprising that generally longer-lived, demersal (bottom) fishes have tended to decline faster than shorter-lived, pelagic (open water) fishes, a trend also indicated by changes in the ratio of piscivorous (mainly demersal) to zooplanktivorous (mainly pelagic) fishes.

It is difficult to fully appreciate the extent of the changes to ecosystems that fishing has wrought, given shifting baselines as to what is considered a pristine ecosystem. These changes, often involving reductions of commercial fish biomasses to a few per cent of their pre-exploitation levels, prevent us taking much guidance from the concept of sustainability, understood as aiming to maintain what we have. Rather, the challenge is rebuilding the stocks in question.

Reducing Fishing Capacity

There is widespread awareness that increases in fishing-fleet capacity represent one of the main threats to the long-term survival of marine capture-fishery resources, and to the fisheries themselves. Reasons advanced for the overcapitalization of the world's fisheries include: the open-access nature of many fisheries; common-pool fisheries that are managed non-cooperatively; sole-ownership fisheries with high discount rates and/or high price-to-cost ratios; the increasing replacement of small-scale fishing vessels with larger ones; and the payment of subsidies by governments to fishers, which generate 'profits' even when resources are overfished.

This literature shows that fishing overcapacity is likely to build up not only under open access, but also under all forms of property regimes. Subsidies, which amount to US$2. 5 billion for the North Atlantic alone, exacerbate the problems arising from the open access and/or 'common pool' aspects of capture fisheries, including fisheries with full-fledged property rights.

Even subsidies used for vessel decommissioning schemes can have negative effects. In fact, decommissioning schemes can lead to the intended reduction in fleet size only if vessel owners are consistently caught by surprise by those offering this form of subsidy. As this is an unlikely proposition, decommissioning schemes often end up providing the collaterals that banks require to underwrite fleet modernizations. Additionally, in most cases, it is not the actual vessel that is retired, but its licence. This means that 'retired' vessels can still be used to catch species without quota (so-called 'under-utilized resources', which are often the prey of species for which there is a quota), or deployed along the coast of some developing country, the access to which may also be subsidized. Clearly, the decommissioning schemes that will have to be implemented if we are ever to reduce overcapacity will have to address these deficiencies if they are not to end up, as most have so far, in fleet modernization and increased fishing mortality.

It is clear that a real, drastic reduction of overcapacity will have to occur if fisheries are to acquire some semblance of sustainability. The required reductions will have to be strong enough to reduce *F* by a factor of two or three in some areas, and even more in others. This must involve even greater decreases in *f*, because catches can be maintained in the face of dwindling biomasses by increasing *q* (and hence F), even when nominal effort is constant. Indeed, this is the very reason behind the incessant technological innovation in fisheries, which now relies on global positioning systems and detailed maps of the sea bottom to seek out residual fish concentrations previously protected by rough terrain. This technological race, and the resulting increase in *q*, is also the reason why fishers often remain unaware of their own impacts on the resource they exploit and object so strongly to scientists' claims of reductions in biomass.

If fleet reduction is done properly, it should result in an increase in net benefits ('rent') from the resources, as predicted by the basic theory of bioeconomics. This can be used, via taxation of the rent gained by the remaining fishers, to ease the transition of those who had to stop fishing. This would contrast with the present situation, where taxes from outside the fisheries sector are used, in form of subsidies, to maintain fishing at levels that are biologically unsustainable, and which ultimately lead to the depletion and collapse of the underlying resources.

Biological Constraints to Fisheries and Aquaculture

Perhaps the strongest factor behind the politicians' use of tax money to subsidize non-sustainable, even destructive fisheries, and its tacit support by the public at large, is the notion that, somehow, the oceans will yield what we need — just because we need it. Indeed, demand projections generated by national and international agencies largely reflect present consumption patterns, which by some means the oceans ought to help us maintain, even if the global human population were to double again. Although much of the deep ocean is indeed unexplored and 'mysterious', we know enough about ocean processes to realize that its productive capacity cannot keep up with an ever-increasing demand for fish.

Just as a tropical scientist might look at the impressive expanse of Canada and assume that this country has boundless potential for agricultural production, unaware that in reality only the thin sliver of land along its southern border (5%) is arable, we terrestrial aliens have assumed that the expanse and depths of the world's oceans will provide for us in the ways that its more familiar coastal fringes have. But this assumption is very wrong. Of the 363 million square kilometres of ocean on this planet, less than 7%—the continental shelves—are shallower than 200 m, and some of this shelf area is covered by ice. Shelves generate the biological production supporting over 90% of global fish catches, the rest consisting of tuna and other oceanic organisms that gather their food from the vast, desert-like expanse of the open oceans.

The overwhelming majority of shelves are now 'sheltered' within the exclusive economic zones (EEZ) of maritime countries, which also include all coral reefs and their fisheries. According to the 1982 United Nations Convention on the Law of the Sea, any country that cannot fully utilize the fisheries resource of its EEZ must make this surplus available to the fleet of other countries. This, along with eagerness for foreign exchange, political pressure and illegal fishing, has led to all of the world's shelves being trawled for bottom fish, purse-seined for pelagic fishes and illuminated to attract and catch squid (to the extent that satellites can map the night time location of fishing fleets as well as that of cities). Overall, about 35% of the primary production on the world's shelves is required to sustain the fisheries, a figure similar to the human appropriation of terrestrial primary production.

The constraints to fisheries expansion that this implies, combined with the declining catches alluded to above, have led to suggestions that aquaculture should be able to bridge the gap between supply and demand. Indeed, the impressive recent growth of reported aquaculture is often cited as evidence of the potential of that sector to meet the growing demand for fish, or even to 'feed the world'.

Three lines of argument suggest that this is unlikely. The first is that the rapidly growing global production figures underlying this documented growth are driven to a large extent by the People's Republic of China, which reported 63% of world aquaculture production in 1998. But it is now known that China not only over-reports its marine fisheries catches, but also the production of many other sectors of its economy. Thus, there is no reason to believe that global aquaculture production in the past decades has risen as much as officially reported.

Second, modern aquaculture practices are largely unsustainable: they consume natural resources at a high rate and, because of their intensity, they are extremely vulnerable to the pollution and disease outbreaks they induce. Thus, shrimp aquaculture ventures are in many cases operated as slash-and-burn operations, leaving devastated coastal habitats and human communities in their wake.

Third, much of what is described as aquaculture, at least in Europe, North America and other parts of the developed world, consists of feedlot operations in which carnivorous fish (mainly salmon, but also various sea bass and other species) are fattened on a diet rich in fish meal and oil. The idea makes commercial sense, as the farmed fish fetch a much higher market price than the fish ground up for fish meal. The point is that operations of this type, which are directed to wealthy consumers, use up much more fish flesh than they produce, and hence cannot replace capture fisheries, especially in developing countries, where very few can afford imported smoked salmon. Indeed, this form of aquaculture represents another source of pressure on wild fish populations.

Perspectives

We believe the concept of sustainability upon which most quantitative fisheries management is based to be flawed, because there is little point in sustaining stocks whose biomass is but a small fraction of its value at the onset of industrial-scale fishing. Rebuilding of marine systems is needed, and we foresee a practical restoration ecology for the oceans that can take place alongside the extraction of marine resources for human food. Reconciling these apparently dissonant goals provides a major challenge for fisheries ecologists, for the public, for management agencies and for the fishing industry. It is important here to realize that there is no reason to expect marine resources to keep pace with the demand that will result from our growing population, and hopefully, growing incomes in now impoverished parts of the world, although we note that fisheries designed to be sustainable in a world of scarcity may be profitable.

We argued in the beginning of this review that whatever semblance of sustainability fisheries in the past might have had was due to their inability to cover the entire range inhabited by the wildlife species that were exploited, which thus had natural reserves. We further argued that the models used traditionally to assess fisheries, and to set catch limits, tend to require explicit knowledge on stock status and total withdrawal from stocks, that is, knowledge that will inherently remain imprecise and error prone. We also showed that generally overcapitalized fisheries are leading, globally, to the gradual elimination of large, long-lived fishes from marine ecosystems, and their replacement by shorter-lived fishes and invertebrates, operating within food webs that are much simplified and lack their former "buffering" capacity.

If these trends are to be reversed, a huge reduction of fishing effort involving effective decommissioning of a large fraction of the world's fishing fleet will have to be implemented, along with fisheries regulations incorporating a strong form of the precautionary principle. The conceptual elements required for this are in place, for example, in form of the FAO Code of Conduct for Responsible Fisheries, but the required political will has been lacking so far, an absence that is becoming more glaring as increasing numbers of fisheries collapse throughout the world, and catches continue to decline.

Given the high level of uncertainty facing the management of fisheries, which induced several collapses, it has been suggested by numerous authors that closing a part of the fishing grounds would prevent overexploitation by setting an upper limit on fishing mortality. Marine protected areas (MPAs), with no-take reserves at their core, combined with a strongly limited effort in the remaining fishable areas, have been shown to have positive effects in helping to rebuild depleted stocks. In most cases, the successful MPAs were used to protect rather sedentary species, rebuild their biomass, and eventually sustain the fishery outside the reserves by exporting juveniles or adults. Although migrating species would not benefit from the local reduction in fishing mortality caused by an MPA, the MPA would still help some of these species by rebuilding the complexity of their habitat destroyed by trawling, and thus decrease mortality of their juveniles. Enforcement of the no-take zones within MPAs would benefit from the application of high technology (for example, satellite monitoring of fishing vessels), presently used mainly to increase fishing pressure.

There is still much fear among fisheries scientists, especially in extra-tropical areas, that the export of fish from such reserves would not be sufficient to compensate for the loss of fishing ground. Although we agree that marine reserves are no panacea, the present trends in fisheries, combined with the low degree of protection presently afforded (only 0.01% of the world's ocean is effectively protected), virtually guarantee that more fish stocks will collapse, and that these collapses will be attributed to environmental fluctuations or climate change. Moreover, many exploited fish populations and eventually fish species will become extinct. MPAs that cover a representative set of marine habitats should help prevent this, just like forest and other natural terrestrial habitats have enabled the survival of wildlife species which agriculture would have otherwise rendered extinct.

Focused studies on the appropriate size and location of marine reserves and their combination into networks, given locale-specific oceanographic conditions, should therefore be supported. This will lead to the identification of reserve designs that would optimize export to adjacent fished areas, and which could thus be offered to the affected coastal and fisher communities, whose consent and support will be required to establish marine reserves and restructure the fisheries. The general public could also be involved, through eco-labelling and other market-driven schemes, and through support for conservation-orientated non-government organizations, which can complement the activities of governmental regulatory agencies.

In conclusion, we think that the restoration of marine ecosystems to some state that existed in the past is a logical policy goal. There is still time to achieve this, and for our fisheries to be put on a path towards sustainability.

REFERENCES

Beverton, R. J. H. & Holt, S. J. *On the Dynamics of Exploited Fish Populations* (Chapman and Hall, London, 1957; Facsimile reprint 1993).

Boyd, R. T. in *Handbook of American Indians: Northwest Coast* (ed. Suttles, W.) 135-148 (Smithsonian Institute, Washington DC, 1990).

Bohnsack, J.A. (Subcommittee Chair) NOAA Tech. Memo. NMFS-SEFC-261 (National Oceanic and Atmospheric Agency, Miami, 1990).

Cushing, D. H. *The Provident Sea* (Cambridge Univ. Press, Cambridge, 1987).

Garcia, S. M. & Newton, C. in Global Trends: Fisheries Management (ed. Sissenwine, M. P.) *Am. Fish. Soc. Symp.* 20, 3-27 (American Fisheries Society, Bethesda, MD, 1997).

Hardy, A. *The Open Sea* (Collins, London, 1956).

Jackson, J. B. C. *et al.* Historical overfishing and the recent collapse of coastal - ecosystems. *Science 293*, 629-638 (2001).

Ludwig, D., Hilbom, R. & Walters, C. Uncertainty, resource exploitation, and conservation: *Lessons* from history. *Science* 260, 17-18 (1993).

Orensanz, J. M. L., Armstrong, J., Armstrong, D. & Hilborn, R. Crustacean resources are vulnerable to serial depletion—the multifaceted decline of crab and shrimp fisheries in the Greater Gulf of Alaska. *Rev. Fish Biol. Fish.* 8, 117-176 (1998).

Pitcher, T. J. Fisheries managed to rebuild ecosystems? Reconstructing the past to salvage the future. *Ecol. Applic.* 11, 601-617 (2001).

Rosenberg, A. A. , Fogarty, M. J. , Sissenwine, M. P. , Beddington, J. R. & Shepherd, J. G. Achieving sustainable use of renewable resources. *Science* 262, 828-829 (1993).

Schaefer, M. B. Some aspects of the dynamics of populations important to the management of the commercial marine fisheries. *Bull. Inter-Am. Trop. Tuna Commiss.* 1,27-56(1954).

Wing, E. S. The sustainability of resources used by native Americans on four Caribbean islands. *Int. J. Osteoarchaeol.* 11, 112-126 (2001).

Yellen, J. E. , Brooks, A. S. , Cornelissen, E. , Mehlman, M. J. & Stewart, K. A middle stone-age worked bone industry from Katanda, Upper Semliki Valley, Zaire. *Science* 268, 553-556 (1995).

Fishery Management
Edited by: Dr. Rabi N. Misra
ISBN: 978-93-5056-789-0
Edition: 2016
Published by: Discovery Publishing House Pvt. Ltd., New Delhi (India)

CHAPTER 15 Conservation and Management of Inland Fishery Resources

Shri G. Chandrayya
Lecturer in Commerce,
Government College (A), Rajahmundry, A.P.
Dr. R.N. Misra
Professor of MBA,
SMIT, Berhampur, Odisha

Current fishery management of inland waters concentrates on three components of the environment/fish/fishery system:

- **Management of the fishery** - regulation oriented activities concerning the activities of the fishers and their social and economic context such as licensing, control of mesh size, setting of closed seasons, control of markets, subsidies, etc. Management policies here should be aimed at: a) limiting access to the fishery so that excess effort is avoided; and b) limiting the use of destructive and harmful fishing gears.
- **Management of the fish** - control over the magnitude and size of the fish population by stocking, introduction of new species and other enhancement techniques as appropriate. Management here is aimed at establishing the most cost-effective approaches for enhancement.
- **Management of the environment** - this is pursued at two different levels: (*a*) negotiating and arranging for adequate

environmental conditions of water quality, quantity, timeliness of flow, habitat diversity etc. ; and (*b*) promoting physical improvements to improve the support capacity for fish

It is evident that of these three process the conventional management of the fishery is limited to the first of these categories.

Management of the fishery itself can be pursued in the framework of sustainability either of the resource as a whole, as in the case where a policy decision is taken to limit fishing severely in the interests of conservation, aesthetics or recreation, or with reference to particular components of the system. Decisions regarding this component of management usually are political and have been made at relatively high level by centralized fisheries agencies in the past. There is now an increasing tendency to involve local peoples in such decisions through co-management or through assignment of rights.

Management of the fish is usually pursued with the direct objective of shaping the fishery to correspond more closely to the requirement of a particular society at a particular time. It is a technical activity pursued at the level of individual fisheries dependent on individual needs. It can only take place, however, if a policy decision is taken to assign the rights to a water body where this type of management is applied so that those investing in the resource can reap the benefits of their investment.

Management of the environment is of two types: firstly interventions which seek to minimize, mitigate or restore from damaging impacts of other users. Here the decisions do not lie with the fishery managers but rather with a larger set of decision makers who implicitly or explicitly allocate the aquatic resource. Secondly, activities which seek to improve the supporting capacity of the ecosystem for fish and which form a complement to biologically-oriented systems of enhancement. Such activities do lie within the purview of the fishery managers although frequently other interests should be consulted before actions such a remeandering, re-creation of gravel bottoms or vegetation control are undertaken.

Within areas under national jurisdiction, States should seek to identify relevant domestic parties having a legitimate interest in the use and management of fisheries resources and establish arrangements for consulting them to gain their collaboration in achieving responsible fisheries.

Parties to inland water management: As the resource is of interest to a large number of players the consultation process should encompass a large section of society. Which elements will be drawn into such discussions will depend on the activities to be contemplated, the geographic area and the social aspirations of the various user groups. Thus, in a tropical river the major dialogue may be between the commercial fishers, the artisanal fishers and those wishing to abstract water for irrigation. In a temperate lake the discourse may be between recreational fishers, wildlife conservationists and water-sport interest groups. The important thing here is that decision makers should recognize those groups having a legitimate call on the aquatic resource and seek to involve them in the consultation process. Where users groups (often the fishers themselves) have no organized voice, mechanisms should be set up to adequately reflect their views.

For transboundary fish stocks, straddling fish stocks, highly migratory fish stocks and high seas fish stocks, where these are exploited by two or more States, the States concerned, including the relevant coastal States in the case of straddling and highly migratory stocks, should co-operate to ensure effective conservation and management of the resources. This should be achieved, where appropriate, through the establishment of a bilateral, subregional or regional fisheries organization or arrangement.

Riverine and diadromous migrants: In inland fisheries the problems posed by the above categories of fish are also met with in the case of the long distance, riverine and diadromous migrants. These species are among the most valuable in a commercial sense but are among the first to disappear when the environment is heavily impacted by dam building, pollution and excessive fishing on the migratory phase. As such, in national and international inland waters alike all measures should be taken to facilitate fish movement past blocking structures such as dams and weirs, to avoid chemical barriers through localised pollution and to prohibit excessive fishing at points where the fish congregate and are especially vulnerable. Protection of migrant species should be a major concern of river basin management authorities.

A subregional or regional fisheries management organization or arrangement should include representatives of States in whose jurisdictions the resources occur, as well as representatives from States which have a real interest in the fisheries or the resources outside national jurisdictions. Where a subregional or regional fisheries management organization or arrangement exists and has the competence to establish conservation and management measures, those States should cooperate by becoming a member of such organization or a participant in such arrangement, and actively participate in its work.

A State which is not a member of a subregional or regional fisheries management organization or is not a participant in a subregional or regional fisheries management arrangement should nevertheless cooperate, in accordance with relevant international agreements and international law, in the conservation and management of the relevant fisheries resources by giving effect to any conservation and management measures adopted by such organization or arrangement.

Representatives from relevant organizations, both governmental and non-governmental, concerned with fisheries should be afforded the opportunity to take part in meetings of subregional and regional fisheries management organizations and arrangements as observers or otherwise, as appropriate, in accordance with the procedures of the organization or arrangement concerned. Such representatives should be given timely access to the records and reports of such meetings, subject to the procedural rules on access to them.

The role of river and lake basin authorities: The articles should be taken to apply equally to river and lake basin authorities charged with the conservation and management of the resources of such basins. Where the prime objectives of such authorities is other than fisheries, for instance power generation, water allocation or navigation, protection of living aquatic resources for biodiversity and fisheries should explicitly be included in their remit.

States should establish, within their respective competencies and capacities, effective mechanisms for fisheries monitoring, surveillance, control and enforcement to ensure compliance with their conservation and management measures, as well as those adopted by subregional or regional organizations or arrangements.

Monitoring, surveillance, control and enforcement: One of the characteristics of inland aquatic systems is their dispersion in space and time. Apart from a few major lakes and rivers, national territories usually contain many thousands of kilometres of stream, many small water bodies, marshes and swamps as well as areas such a rice fields which are used for rearing or capture offish. The dispersion of the resource is mirrored in an equal diffusion of fishing areas and fish landings. This means that comprehensive monitoring, surveillance, control and enforcement of all inland fisheries within a national territory is frequently beyond the capacity of a State. The most economical solution to this is to charge the fishers themselves with the policing and record keeping functions of the fishery and to empower them through legal and protected rights to the resource to carry out this function.

Control of effort: Apart for a few major fisheries on large lakes and rivers, inland fisheries are generally pursued with many small artisanal units rather than single large craft. In these cases, and because of the diffuseness of the fishery and landings discussed above, it is difficult to control access to the fishery directly. For many, fishing is a part-time occupation and measures of effort are difficult to obtain. Furthermore, in rivers and fluctuating lakes the yield to be expected from the fishery may vary enormously from year-to-year. In this context absolutes are difficult to establish and most traditional management systems have developed mechanisms to deal with the variability and with the control of access. For this reason it is advisable to establish co-management or local management systems that can better deal with the local conditions. Where enhancement is adopted as a major approach to development and management of the fishery, access should be more strictly controlled and limited to those investing directly in the development of the resource. This implies some fixing of exploitation rights that may cause local inequities. Social and economic impacts of such decisions therefore should be well studied before they are adopted.

States and subregional or regional fisheries management organizations and arrangements should ensure transparency in the mechanisms for fisheries management and in the related decision-making process.

States and subregional or regional fisheries management organizations and arrangements should give due publicity to conservation and management measures and ensure that laws, regulations and other legal rules governing their implementation are effectively disseminated. The bases and purposes of such measures should be explained to users of the resource in order to facilitate their application and thus gain increased support in the implementation of such measures.

Management Objectives

Recognizing that long-term sustainable use of fisheries resources is the overriding objective of conservation and management, States and subregional or regional fisheries management organizations and arrangements should, inter alia, adopt appropriate measures, based on the best scientific evidence available, which are designed to maintain or restore stocks at levels capable of producing maximum sustainable yield, as qualified by relevant environmental and economic factors, including the special requirements of developing countries.

Sustainability and inland ecosystems: Most inland aquatic ecosystems have already been substantially altered by the activities of man. The long historical process of dam construction, draining of marginal wetlands and straightening, deepening and encasing major channels has modified the original pristine situation of most rivers on most continents. Lakes have been less affected although eutrophication, acidification and siltation have also substantially altered their character. Further changes have arisen from species introductions. In some cases the success of introduced species resulted from physical modifications of the system which selected against native species. In other cases a mix of species suited to colonize new water bodies such as reservoirs were introduced as native species were unable to adapt to the new environments. Issues of sustainability in inland waters have, therefore, to be viewed against a background of change which has affected most waters of the world. This does not mean that sustainability is not achievable but it does mean that the baseline has changed and that very often sustainability has to be pursued against a background of new species and altered habitats. Strategies should, therefore, be based on this assumption rather than on vain attempts to restore a substantially altered ecological balance.

Such measures should provide inter alia that:

(*a*) *excess fishing capacity is avoided and exploitation of the stocks remains economically viable;*

Measures for the conservation and sustainable management of inland fisheries can only be effective if excessive fishing effort is avoided. In order to control fishing capacity access must be controlled although technological solutions through improved enhancement practices and more environmentally friendly fishing gears can also be adopted.

(*b*) *the economic conditions under which fishing industries operate promote responsible fisheries;*

Access to inland resources: Many different types of access pattern exist in inland waters. These range from outright private ownership in the case of small lakes and ponds, through communal ownership to state ownership. In many cases the inland resource is thought of as open access and fishing has often provided an occupation of last resort, especially for landless peoples. In areas liable to periodic drought inland resources may also treated as famine crops and the resource is heavily exploited until better food supplies return. More frequently, however, access or fishing rights are determined by traditional allocation of the resource among riverain peoples. In some cases fishing rights are acquired through licenses issued by the state or purchased from the owners either directly or through auction. In systems where there is a stable system of exploitation rights assigned over long periods it is in the interest of the fishers to manage the resource sustainably. However, should the assigned period be too short, especially in fisheries where rights are acquired by auction, there is a tendency for the operator to attempt to recuperate his costs as quickly as possible by overly intensive fishing. Consequently assignment of rights either directly or through mechanisms such as auction should be for as long a period as possible.

(c) *the interests of fishers, including those engaged in subsistence, small-scale and artisanal fisheries, are taken into account.*

Inland fisheries are essentially small-scale, subsistence or artisanal in nature. It is not unusual for small-scale commercial, artisanal and subsistence fisheries to co-exist in the same area although with some degree of conflictuality. Major impacts on fishers usually derive from outside the fisheries sector when large scale projects involving alternative uses of water can alter the whole nature of the resource. Typical of this is the need to displace communities and re-educate fishers when riverine fisheries are converted to lacustrine ones following impoundment. The impacts on and needs of fishers should be taken into account within the general impact assessments of all such projects.

(d) *biodiversity of aquatic habitats and ecosystems is conserved and endangered species are protected.*

(e) *depleted stocks are allowed to recover or, where appropriate, are actively restored.*

Conservation of biological diversity: The comments develop the theme that existing biological diversity in inland waters has been eroded by a large number of species introductions, by stocking programmes and by environmental changes induced by human activities. It is therefore difficult to establish criteria for future conservation efforts. Apart from a few directed attempts to rehabilitate rivers and lakes and restore historically appropriate faunas most efforts at conservation have to concentrate on maintaining the sustainability of vastly altered species assemblages in modified aquatic ecosystems. In this case the responsibility of the fisheries manager is to ensure that further degradation does not occur through additional introductions of inappropriate species, that the genetic composition of stocked fish is compatible with the native stocks and, above all, that the environment is protected from further negative impacts.

Protection of endangered species and habitats: Conservation problems are not limited to endangered species but also to certain types of wetland habitat. The options for species conservation are *ex situ* whereby the threatened species are kept in aquaria or other suitable localities with the eventual objective of reintroduction to the native water when conditions permit. This strategy is particularly popular for smaller ornamental species although many larger species are held in aquaculture installations or have been introduced outside their original range for this purpose. Ideally such options should not only be adopted for species but for particularly valuable strains in order to maintain the genetic diversity of the species. *In situ* conservation implies one of three strategies. Firstly programmes of stocking the subject species into native waters where self-reproducing stocks have failed for one reason or another. Secondly through the establishment of reserves. In lakes areas may be set aside as protected locations although such reserves will only serve as protection against fishing or direct environmental interventions. They will not protect against diffuse influences such a eutrophication or the introduction of a major predator. In rivers the concept of a chain of beads pattern of reserves has been developed whereby it is deemed ecologically sufficient to allow selected areas along the river to retain their natural flood regime and floodplain morphology. Unfortunately the cumulative effects of flood control and modification in the system as a whole may place undue hydraulic stresses on such locations and solutions to this have to be sought. The third strategy, the complete rehabilitation of the system, is at present confined to smaller lakes and rivers.

(f) adverse environmental impacts on the resources from human activities are assessed and, where appropriate, corrected.

Environmental impacts: Much of current concern with inland waters revolves around various types of environmental damage. There are strong trends to try to reverse the sometimes long standing adverse impacts in more affluent temperate nations. However, the pressure to expand negatively-impacting activities such as dam building, creation of navigation channels, water abstraction for irrigation, and pollution by urban, agricultural and industrial wastes is still prevalent in developing economies. Because the short and medium-term economic benefits of such developments to the country are seen to be far superior to the maintenance of the environment and the fishery resources there is a strong temptation to give conservation of the aquatic resource relatively low priority. This may be viewed as a subsidy to development on the part of the environment. Experience has shown, however, that this debt has to be repaid as many valuable, but so far uncosted, ecosystem services disappear along with the health of the environment. States should therefore endeavour to plan forward through impact assessments and investment in mitigating measures as an integral part of development.

(g) pollution, waste, discards, catch by lost or abandoned gear, catch of non-target species, both fish and non-fish species, and impacts on associated or dependent species are minimized, through measures including, to the extent practicable, the development and use of selective, environmentally safe and cost-effective fishing gear and techniques.

Damaging fishing methods: In multi-species fisheries many fishing methods are judged by the fishers to be detrimental to the fishery as a whole or to the fish stock. In traditional fishery management systems such gears are usually banned for the whole or part of the year. With the breakdown of traditional systems of fisheries management in many parts of the world the use of such gear has remained unchecked and managers should seek to limit their use as appropriate. Certain fishing methods are universally recognized as constituting a menace to the fishery, for example fishing with explosives, poisons or electric gear, and these should be banned in all inland waters except, in certain circumstances for scientific research. Equally cross river barrier traps set for migrating fish at their areas of maximum concentration should never exceed two-thirds of the channel width to allow for a percentage of escapees.

States should assess the impacts of environmental factors on target stocks and species belonging to the same ecosystem or associated with or dependent upon the target stocks, and assess the relationship among the populations in the ecosystem.

Management Framework and Procedures

To be effective, fisheries management should be concerned with the whole stock unit over its entire area of distribution and take into account previously agreed management measures established and applied in the same region, all removals and the biological unity and other biological characteristics of the stock. The best scientific evidence available should be used to determine, inter alia, the area of distribution of the resource and the area through which it migrates during its life cycle.

The nature of multi-species fisheries: Fish assemblages in rivers and many lakes are highly complex. The number of species in a river or lake is strongly correlated with its basin area. As fishing effort increases characteristic and predictable changes occur in the fish assemblages which have strong implications for sustainability and management. In general as effort increases larger individuals and species disappear from the assemblage to be replaced by smaller counterparts. This means a gradual drift downwards in mean length of the target populations, towards shorter lived, faster growing species. This is accompanied by an initial increase and later a decrease in the number of species in the exploitable population although the number of fish actually appearing in the catch will increase until a certain critical level is passed. Standing stocks will decrease but total production will rise giving an increase in the ratio of production to biomass. As a result, although individual species in the assemblage may conform to standard surplus yield models, the overall catch curve rises initially to reach a plateau which is sustained over a considerable range of increasing effort. Eventually, when effort reaches sufficiently high levels the assemblage may become sufficiently impoverished as to become destabilized and collapse but more frequently economic factors limit the rise in effort and prevent this level of overfishing. Very high effort fisheries are usually the result of high population densities brought about by local economic expansions. These in themselves tend to place pressure on the resource through the pollution and environmental modification. Changes in fish assemblages subject to such stresses parallel those produced by fishing and the combined effects of fishing and environmental degradation may well be synergistic.

There are several implications for management in this process. Firstly, classical terms such as overfishing are difficult to apply. Individual species may be overfished and disappear from the fishery but the assemblage as a whole continues to produce at a high level, albeit of fish which may not have the same value as those that have disappeared. In this context overfishing can only be deemed to occur with reference to some defined value such as a particular group of species, quality, size etc. Secondly, the fishery can absorb increased amounts of effort, either as labour or as improved technology than would be supported by a fishery concentrating on only the larger species in the assemblage. These two factors mean that those responsible for managing the fishery can select either explicitly or implicitly from a range of options between aiming the fishery at only the most valuable larger species, through maximizing yield but retaining a reasonable quality of product, or to maximizing the employment (or distribution of the benefits of the fishery) by allowing the effort to rise. In reality it is not uncommon to see fisheries managed for a combination of these objectives.

In order to conserve and manage transboundary fish stocks, straddling fish stocks, highly migratory fish stocks and high seas fish stocks throughout their range, conservation and management measures established for such stocks in accordance with the respective competences of relevant States or, where appropriate, through subregional and regional fisheries management organizations and arrangements, should be compatible. Compatibility should be achieved in a manner consistent with the rights, competences and interests of the States concerned.

Long-term management objectives should be translated into management actions, formulated as a fishery management plan or other management framework.

Allocation of the aquatic resource: States should clearly formulate national plans for the use of water including allocation for fisheries and for the protection of the aquatic environment. Within the fisheries sector objectives should be individually set for major fisheries and fisheries management strategies developed accordingly. Smaller rivers and lakes may be grouped by regional objectives within the country. Decisions need to be taken on use -normal capture or enhanced fisheries.

Target species - fisheries concentrating only on larger species, or maximum production of larger numbers of smaller species. Allocation -recreational fisheries, fisheries reserved for native peoples, open access or restricted access for commercial purposes, etc.

States and, where appropriate, subregional or regional fisheries management organizations and arrangements should foster and promote international co-operation and co-ordination in all matters related to fisheries, including information gathering and exchange, fisheries research, management and development.

Basin management for shared basins:

States seeking to take any action through a non-fishery organization which may affect the conservation and management measures taken by a competent subregional or regional fisheries management organization or arrangement should consult with the latter, in advance to the extent practicable, and take its views into account.

Multi-purpose management: As a multiple resource system with a heavy economic bias to non-fishery uses of the aquatic system most management decisions regarding the development of the basin are taken by organizations outside the fisheries sector. This means that the fishery is called on to manage its resource under the constraints imposed by others. This clearly calls for full consultation with other users in an attempt to negotiate optimum conditions for fisheries interests. Increasingly, however, external constraints are not only imposed by economic interests but by conservationist and cultural groupings including animal rights and environmentalist groups. Very often the agenda of these groups contrasts with that of fisheries but on occasions their interests may coincide when there is a powerful need for conservation in the face of abuse of the environment. In such circumstances alliances should be sought with other groupings of parallel interest to form a stronger bargaining position. The concept of integrated aquatic resource management has been developed in an attempt to provide a set of tools for interested parties to jointly plan the allocation and responsibility for the management of all resources in a basin. This requires that appropriate which are competent and mandated to represent these interests groupings exist. In many countries such groupings either do not exist or the official recognition that would enable them to effectively participate in such discussions. States should endeavour to encourage the development of representative user groups for this purpose.

Data Gathering and Management Advice

When considering the adoption of conservation and management measures, the best scientific evidence available should be taken into account in order to evaluate the current state of the fishery resources and the possible impact of the proposed measures on the resources.

Impact assessment: Systematic impact assessments should be made of all projects including proposals for change of land use, deforestation etc. which have the potential to alter the aquatic ecosystem and the fisheries that depend on it. Such assessments should equally be made of proposals for mitigation or rehabilitation projects. Impact assessments should then be taken into account when planning the overall allocation of the aquatic system between fisheries and other users. The fact that the cumulative effects of many small projects may equal or exceed that of one big one should be taken into account in considering impacts.

Research in support of fishery conservation and management should be promoted, including research on the resources and on the effects of climatic, environmental and socio-economic factors. The results of such research should be disseminated to interested parties.

Research: The difficulties of researching inland waters because of their diffuse and discrete nature have already been commented on in section 6. 4. At the level of species and ecosystems knowledge on inland water resources is variable and patchy. Some systems, such as temperate salmonid streams, are well understood whereas in others, such as large tropical rivers the taxonomy, biology and ecology of the numerous species is very incomplete. Black box models which require only limited knowledge of the individual species involved have been used widely in fisheries management and these function well within the very general limits of their application. More detailed planning for the conservation of individual species, the rehabilitation of rivers for specific faunas or the consideration of proposals for species introductions requires more complete knowledge of the species involved. Equally, evaluation of impacts of activities such as dam construction, water abstraction, channelization etc. presupposes knowledge of specific aspects of the biology of the fish likely to be affected including migration patterns, breeding behaviour, feeding requirements, instream flow needs etc. Research requirements are not limited to the biological disciplines as. On the whole, the social and economic dimensions of the sector are equally poorly understood. Here more information is needed on user group performance, behaviour, interactions and allocation of benefits.

Studies should be promoted which provide an understanding of the costs, benefits and effects of alternative management options designed to rationalise fishing, in particular, options relating to excess fishing capacity and excessive levels of fishing effort.

Economics of inland fisheries: The economics of inland fisheries operations are generally poorly understood. The diversity within an individual fishery, the strong seasonality, the year-to-year variation of many fisheries, the fact that many fishers are part time moving between fishing and other activities, and the complexity of the diffuse marketing structures through which most inland catches are passed on to the consumer all complicate such studies. More information is needed so that more appropriate management policies be formulated with due consideration being given to allocation and distributional aspects. Two sectors in particular are attracting interest in this respect, the cost effectiveness of enhanced fisheries and the economics of recreational fishing.

The cost effectiveness of enhancements: Activities to improve fisheries have a long history and stocking in particular has become a universal management tool. These practises have, however, usually been adopted uncritically with little attempt to determine their economic effectiveness. Enhancement has now reached a level where increasing adoption of techniques such as stocking, and the increased privatization of such fisheries means that margins for waste are considerably reduced. States and other agencies involved in fisheries management should carefully evaluate the practices to reduce waste and improve their cost-effectiveness with a view to ensuring their financial sustainability.

Valuation of recreational fishery: Recreational fisheries present a special case within the set of fisheries in that practitioners do not rely on the activity for their livelihood and that many of the terms in calculating their value lie outside the fishery itself. Recreational fishers are usually prepared to spend considerable sums of money on their sport not only in licenses for access to the fishery but for gear, transport and accommodation.

Groups of resource owners, professional assistants, boat owners, etc. may, depend on the recreational fishery for their livelyhood and the recreational fishery may thus contribute significantly to local economies through its employment potential. In this way the product of the fishery in terms of fish is only of small significance and other aspects of the fishery such as aesthetic enjoyment and local economics become more important. There are several methods to assess the economic value of goods and services supplied by nature in the absence of a market. Whereas a market, and thus price, usually exists for food fish, the recreational value of the fishery resource may need to be assessed through non-market valuation techniques which indirectly or directly attempt to measure the users' willingness-to-pay.

For example, based on expenditures and travel behaviour (travel-cost valuation method), it has often been found that the willingness-to-pay for the fishery resource by recreational fishers is higher by an order of magnitude than its value based on the market price of food fish. Production cost estimates may also be of value in that the cost of material for stocking may often exceed that which can be economically supported by a food fishery. These comparisons, however, are not without problems, especially in many developing countries where on the one hand, the market price of food fish may only inaccurately reflect real food fish demand because many consumers may be unable to indicate their willingness-to-pay in the market due to poverty and, on the other, where a greatly unequal income distribution 'inflates' the expenditures which some sections of the society can incur for recreational purposes. Whatever the context, however, recreational fisheries, where they become established, tend to drive out purely food fisheries because of their apparent greater value and the greater political influence of the recreational fishery lobby.

States should ensure that timely, complete and reliable statistics on catch and fishing effort are collected and maintained in accordance with applicable international standards and practices and in sufficient detail to allow sound statistical analysis. Such data should be updated regularly and verified through an appropriate system. States should compile and disseminate such data in a manner consistent with any applicable confidentiality requirements.

Inland fisheries statistics: The number and dispersion of lakes, reservoirs and rivers within the territory of any nation is such that it is difficult to set up adequate sampling systems to cover the whole of the resource, nor is it generally economic to establish expensive sampling stations on numerous small water bodies which have little individual production. Two major solutions to this have been adopted. Firstly to have official concern only for the most significant landing sites on the largest rivers and lakes. This technique tends to ignore a substantial part of the national resource because, although the individual yields from small rivers and lakes may be insignificant the cumulative contribution to national catches may be high. Secondly, to base statistical collection on a weighted sampling frame which aims at being representative for the country as a whole and thirdly, to increasingly rely on fisherman's groups to participate in the collection and reporting of fishery data.

Essential components of statistical analysis: The temptation to be overly comprehensive in data collection should be avoided and certain basic parameters should be selected as the basis for statistical programmes. These may vary according to the type of fishery. For instance, in a simple capture fishery data on effort, catch, length analysis and species composition should be enough to characterise the fishery. In enhanced fisheries more detailed information on input and rates of return will be needed. The measures for recreational fisheries may differ depending on whether the catch is consumed, removed or returned. They should also include such factors as angler satisfaction which do not figure in the more general statistics. In any case recreational fishers as a whole are more willing to collaborate in gathering information which may improve their sport and the obligation to report is often included in the license.

In order to ensure sustainable management of fisheries and to enable social and economic objectives to be achieved, sufficient knowledge of social, economic and institutional factors should be developed through data gathering, analysis and research.

Studies on the social component of the fishery: Remarks on the knowledge of the economics of inland fisheries also apply to social issues as the two factors are usually highly related. In the past many fisheries were regulated by tradition through established hierarchies of responsibility. Many such systems disappeared or became degraded because traditional rights remained unprotected and uncodified. As a consequence, the entry of new commercial and recreational users created quasi open access which impaired the benefits which the traditional artisanal fishers would normally have obtained from their fishery. Knowledge of the functioning of such systems is important as attempts to re-establish co-management systems rely to a large measure on re-establishing similar mechanisms. Of particular importance in social studies are the mechanisms whereby societies adapt to shifts in management strategy within multi-gear multi-community fisheries, to changes in overall use patterns particularly the conversion of rivers to reservoirs following damming, to changes in ownership and access patterns within fishery enhancement programmes etc.

States should compile fishery-related and other supporting scientific data relating to fish stocks covered by subregional or regional fisheries management organizations or arrangements in an internationally agreed format and provide them in a timely manner to the organization or arrangement. In cases of stocks which occur in the jurisdiction of more than one State and for which there is no such organization or arrangement, the States concerned should agree on a mechanism for co-operation to compile and exchange such data.

Regional fishery statistics: While most inland rivers and lakes lie within the confines of one state many major lakes and rivers are international in that their waters lie within more than one national territory. Collection of statistics and data has normally been regarded a national concern except in a few international water bodies where a competent basin authority exists. Problems of consistency of reporting and interpretation have therefore become a problem. The need for more unified approaches to inland fisheries conservation and management, especially in international rivers and lakes has given rise to a degree of synthesis which has formulated general principles of system function but the application of these principles to individual systems remains to be generalized. Added to this, there is at present no separate reporting of inland production in the national statistics of many countries which means that it difficult to estimate the global or regional contribution of fish from natural inland systems to global fish production, to analyse the contribution of different production systems to the production and to detect trends in resource use. The improvement of collection and reporting of inland catch statistics and related information and the harmonization of methods for doing so is therefore high priority in many areas.

Index

J

K

L

M

N

O

P